In The
TIGER JUNGLE

And Other Stories
of Missionary Work Among
the Telugus of India

In The
TIGER JUNGLE

And Other Stories
of Missionary Work Among
the Telugus of India

BY THE REV. JACOB CHAMBERLAIN, M.D., D.D.

A MISSIONARY OF THE REFORMED CHURCH
OF AMERICA, AT MADANAPALLE, INDIA.

WITH AN INTRODUCTION BY THE
REV. FRANCIS E. CLARK, D.D.

CHAMBERLAIN, JACOB (1835-1908)
In The Tiger Jungle (1896).—

Modern Edition © 2018 Full Well Ventures

ISBN-13: 978-1-62834-022-8

ISBN-10: 1-62834-022-3

AUTHOR'S DEDICATION

To her

WHO FOR THIRTY-SEVEN YEARS

HAS SHARED MY LABORS AND MY JOYS

AND WHO SHARES THEM STILL.

TABLE OF CONTENTS

INTRODUCTION BY THE REV. F.E. CLARK, D.D.   11

PREFACE, BY THE AUTHOR.   15

PRELIMINARY: WHO ARE THESE TELUGUS?   17

I. IN THE TIGER JUNGLE: DOES GOD HEAR PRAYER?   23

II. THE MAN WITH THE WONDERFUL BOOKS.   39

III. ENCOUNTER WITH A TEN-FOOT SERPENT, AND ITS RESULTS.   47

IV. THE GOSPEL RIVER IN INDIA: HOW IT FLOWS.   53

V. THE GOSPEL RIVER IN INDIA: THE "GOSPEL IN SONG."   59

VI. THE GOSPEL RIVER IN INDIA: THE FLEET-FOOTED TRACT.   67

VII. ESTABLISHING A NEW STATION: VARIETIES IN MISSION WORK.   75

VIII. GOSPEL PREACHING TOURS.   85

IX. GOSPEL PREACHING AT HINDU FAIRS.   91

X. TREATED WITH A SHOWER OF STONES.   99

XI. A FRUITFUL PREACHING TOUR.   103

XII. OUR VILLAGE CATHEDRAL.   119

XIII.	THE BUILDING AND OPENING OF A FREE READING ROOM AT MADANAPALLE.	127
XIV.	A BRAHMAN ON THE BIBLE.	137
XV.	THE VILLAGE MAGISTRATE'S DEATH.	143
XVI.	NARASAPPA'S MOTHER; OR, CHRIST'S HIDDEN ONLINE	147
XVII.	AN AUDIENCE OF MONKEYS.	151
XVIII.	THE STICK-TO-IT MISSIONARY.	155
XIX.	UNHATCHABLE INK BOTTLES; OR, TAUGHT BY A HEN.	161
XX.	WINDING UP A HORSE.	165
XXI.	BAPTISM OF A BRAHMAN.	175
XXII.	BÍMGÁNI RÁMANNA; OR, UNRECKONED FRUITS.	179
XXIII.	THE MARGOSA TREE AND THE HINDU TEMPLE.	183

ILLUSTRATIONS

A Noted Banyan Tree, Page 52.

Section of Banyan Tree,
Showing its Mode of Growth, Page 84.

A Hindu Village, Page 98.

Group of Hindu Idols,
Out of Employment, Page 118.

Native Christian Wedding Group, Page 142

The Mission Church, Madanapalle,
Page 154

The Gopurams of a Hindu Temple, Page
174

Introduction

I have long held the opinion, and often expressed it, that the young people of our land need not patronize the dime novel or the "penny dreadful" to find stirring adventure and thrilling narrative.

There is one source which furnishes stories of intense and dramatic interest, abounding in novel situations and spiced with abundant adventure; and this source is at the same time the purest and most invigorating fountain at which our youth can drink.

To change the figure, this is a mine hitherto largely unworked; it contains rich nuggets of ore, which will well repay the prospector in this new field.

I know of no one better fitted to delve in this mine and bring this rich ore to the surface than the author of this book. For many years a missionary in India, the fairy-land of romance, a fascinating writer, a lover of youth, one who knows how to make even a commonplace story interesting and an interesting story fascinating— who could better write a book of missionary adventure than Dr. Jacob Chamberlain?

Already scores of articles from his pen have appeared in our leading religious periodicals, by whose readers they are eagerly sought; and some of them have obtained an immense circulation in leaflet form. They have stirred the imagination and quickened the missionary zeal of a multitude of people.

The very titles of these chapters engage the attention of every reader: "In the Tiger Jungle," "Winding up a Horse," "Encounter with a Ten-foot Serpent," "The Stick-to-it Missionary," "An Audience of Monkeys," and others no less striking.

What young person could read these titles without desiring to know something more of this charming book? But the best of this volume does not lie in the taking titles of its chapters, in its fascinating style, or in the stirring adventure which it narrates; it lies in the genuine missionary fervor, which cannot but impart itself to those who peruse it, and in the realistic and vivid pictures of missionary life, which make the countries described, and their people, and the work done for them live again in the glowing printed page.

I believe that this book will increase the host of consecrated young men and women who will be willing to devote their lives to the Master's service in far-off lands. It will kindle anew the fires of devotion in the hearts of a vastly larger multitude who must stay at home and do their missionary work in America. It will prompt the desire of many to give largely and regularly to the great cause of world-wide missions, in order that they may be at work on both sides of the globe for the one Master twenty-four hours in every day — personally in their own land, and through their representative in some land across the sea. It will face every reader with the demand that he or she must " go or send." It will make missions a real and living thing to a multitude to whom it is now a misty dream of heroic service. It is a book which may well be placed in every Sunday-school library, which should be owned by every Christian Endeavor Society and mission circle, which many Christian parents and teachers will find admirably suited for a Christmas or birthday present, and which, wherever it goes, will carry its own lesson and its own welcome.

FRANCIS E. CLARK.
BOSTON, JULY 20, 1896.

PREFACE

URGENT requests from many sources, some from personal friends, others from entire strangers, by letter and in person, that there might be issued in book form a collection of sketches and other articles which have appeared from my pen in a wide range of periodicals in America and other lands during the past years, have led me, on the eve of my return to India, to prepare such a collection, only to find that I had gathered far more material than should appear in one volume. I have therefore selected a small portion of the material I had prepared, and present it in this volume. My selection may not always have been wise; in fact, I have not brought in one half of the articles that have been specially asked for, lest the book be so bulky as to be forbidding. That can, however, be remedied by the issue of another series, should it be called for. I have also in preparation a more pretentious work on India and the Hindus, which, if God spare my life, I hope to be able after a time to present to those interested in the Orient.

This little volume I now send forth with the fervent prayer that God would so use these simple sketches as only to glorify His own holy name and advance His cause and kingdom at the ends of the earth.

JACOB CHAMBERLAIN.

JACOB CHAMBERLAIN

Preliminary:
Who Are These Telugus?

The Hindus of today are not the original inhabitants of India. In the earlier ages the peninsula of India was sparsely populated by a race whom we may consider the aborigines, who were smaller of stature and darker of color, who had no written language, and of whom we know but little.

About the time of Abraham the tribes of Central Asia began to migrate. The Dravidian tribes pushed through the mountains into India, and, pressing on southward, occupied what is now the Madras Presidency, together with parts of Bombay and the native kingdoms of Hyderabad, Mysore, and Travancore. These immigrants are spoken of in Sanskrit literature as the *pancha Dravida*, or the " five Dravidian tribes." They were distinct tribes, each having its own language, its own customs, and its own independent organization. They seem, however, to have been federated and working in harmony, all seeking for new homes in a more genial clime.

The Tamil tribe was in the forefront, and did not rest until its advance-guard had reached Cape Comorin, at the southern extremity of India. They occupied the country from that point northward four hundred miles to Madras, and in width from the Bay of Bengal to the Western Ghats, or mountains, which, like a backbone, reach from south to north fifty to one hundred miles distant from the shores of the Sea of Arabia.

To the west of these Western Ghats, between them and the sea, the Malayálim people located, occupying what is now the kingdom of Travancore. They are less in number than the Tamils and are closely allied to them.

North of them, on the Sea of Arabia and stretching out over the modern kingdom of Mysore, the Kanarese tribe found its abode. They number more than the Malayálims, but less than the Tamils.

The Telugu tribe came last. They occupied the region lying on the Bay of Bengal, from Madras north to Ganjam, and westward to and including part of Mysore and the most of Hyderabad, a region more than five hundred miles long and two to three hundred miles broad, while the Maráthis occupied the region westward of them all, up the coast of the Arabian Sea. Other tribes followed on and occupied all North India. The Telugus are the most numerous of all the Dravidian peoples, numbering at the present time between eighteen and twenty millions.

Still later, in the time between Moses and David, there came another immigration into India from the higher table-lands of Asia.

The Aryans, our ancestors, were seized with the spirit of migration. One division went westward into Europe and became the progenitors of the Greeks, the Latins, the Saxons, and the English. The other division sought for more southern climes, and, pressing through the Himalayan mountain-passes, first settled in North India and then gradually spread themselves through all the country, not as conquerors, but in comity among the other peoples.

The Dravidian tribes had brought their own fairly well

cultivated languages with them, and a religion, of which little is now known. The Aryans brought with them the Sanskrit language, the elder and more ornate sister of the Greek and the Latin. They brought also the Vedas, their scriptures, and the Hinduism which is inculcated in the Vedas. The Vedas taught in the main a pure monotheism, and gave essentially true ideas of God and man and sin and sacrifice.

About the time of their arrival in North India, however, there was evolved a second series of religious books, the Upanisháds, or commentaries on the Vedas, the Shastras, and later the Puránas. In these appeared the first glimmerings of the Hindu triad, Brahma, Vishnu, and Siva, with their host of attendant minor gods; then first appeared the system of caste.

The Aryans divided themselves into three castes: the Brahmans, created, as they taught, from the brain of Brahma; the Kshatriyas, or soldier caste, created by a subsequent act of Brahma, from his shoulders; the Vaisyas, or merchant and artisan caste, from his loins. Of the Dravidians and other earlier immigrants they constituted the great fourth caste, the Sudras, whom they declared to have been created by Brahma from his thighs. They were to be the farmers, mechanics, and laborers. They are subdivided into more than forty distinct castes, who will not eat together nor intermarry. Those who remained of the still earlier inhabitants, the aborigines, became the Pariahs in South India, with similar non-caste people in the other portions of the country.

Caste is thus a religious distinction, not a social. There was a different creation of each. If their system be admitted, the Brahman may justly say to the others, "Stand by thyself;

come not near me, for I am holier than thou." This caste system is one of the greatest barriers to the introduction of the religion of Jesus, which proclaims to the proud Brahman that " God hath made of one blood all nations of men."

The Brahmans mingled among all the other peoples of India, and from their superior education and mental power soon gained an ascendancy and succeeded in inducing all the earlier peoples to accept their religion and their caste system. They became the sacerdotal class, the priests and school-teachers of all India. They did not attempt to intro-duce their language, the Sanskrit, except as the language of ritual, but themselves adopted for daily use and further cultivated the languages of the Tamils, the Telugus, the Kanarese, and others of the preceding immigrants among whom they resided.

The religion which they introduced taught of the Hindu triad, Brahma the Creator, Vishnu the Preserver, and Siva the Destroyer, and a host of other gods, theoretically inferior to the triad, but with practically much greater influence over the daily lives and the welfare of the people. These minor gods are far more feared and far more worshiped by the people than the triad. They hold that there are three hun-dred and thirty millions of gods, male and female, named and unnamed, and the country is filled with shrines and temples, in which are images of multitudes of these gods, or idols, to receive the homage, the worship, the sacrifices, of the people.

The Brahmans further taught the doctrine of transmi-gration, which is that at death the soul simply passes on one stage in its existence to be born again in another body—in a higher order if he had done more good than evil, in a lower if the evil had exceeded the good. If, after countless transmigrations, the account of evil were canceled by the amount of good deeds performed, and sufficient merit were attained, the soul would then be absorbed into that of the Deity, and individual existence would cease. This is their doctrine of Nirvana, or final absorption, which is the highest goal to which a Hindu can attain.

To obtain the needed merit a system of duties is prescribed. It consists of the daily and strict observance of all caste rules, the performance of the prescribed acts of worship, sacrifices, ablutions, pilgrimages to holy shrines, bathing in the sacred rivers, penances, self-torture, hermit life apart from one's kind in complete isolation in a desert; and thus it is hoped that the transmigrations of the soul will be brought to a speedier end and Nirvana be attained. The mass of the people, however, are content with the daily observance of caste rules and the abundant worship of their multitudinous idols.

This very brief outline of the Hinduism of to-day would be incomplete without the further statement that vast numbers of Hindus, now educated in Western learning, no longer at heart hold to the system of modern Hinduism as above outlined, although they still outwardly conform to the rules of caste and of ritual. There is an unrest among all the educated classes and a looking for something different. Some are seeking a revival of ancient Vedic Hinduism, an essentially pure monotheism, with no caste, no idolatry, no senseless ritual. Others are seeking an eclectic system, aiming to obtain the morality and uplifting influence observed in Christianity without accepting Christ. Others, in vast numbers, are veering away into blank agnosticism. All these maintain an outwardly very hostile attitude toward evangelical Christianity. There is nevertheless a quiet, unobserved undercurrent among very many toward an open acceptance of Jesus of Nazareth as the Saviour of the whole world.

This condition of unrest, of the expectancy of some change soon to come, which is freely admitted even in the native newspapers, both in English and in the vernaculars, gives a golden opportunity for pressing the claims of Christianity upon the people of India at the present juncture. It emphasizes the terrible responsibility resting on the church of Christ, lest this God-given opportunity pass by, never to be repeated.

For more than a third of a century I have been engaged in pressing this work among the Telugu people, of whom I have given some account above, and the following pages contain incidents, most of them jotted down at the time, which have occurred in connection with my missionary labors among these Telugus.

I. In The Tiger Jungle:
Does God Hear Prayer?

It was in September, 1863. I was taking a long exploring, preaching, and Bible-distributing journey up through the native kingdom of Hyderabad and on into Central India, where no missionary had ever before worked. It .was a journey of twelve hundred miles on horseback, of four to five months, and through a region little known and difficult to traverse, and by many regarded as exceedingly dangerous. Indeed, before starting I had received messages and letters from numbers of missionaries and laymen, warning me of the danger, and begging me not to throw away my life and end disastrously a missionary career so near its beginning.

I had surveyed the danger, measured the obstacles, and counted the cost, and considering none of them sufficient to cancel the command, "Go ye into all the world," I had covenanted for the journey with the " I will be with you always," and started on my way. I was accompanied by four native assistants, picked men from the larger number who had volunteered to be my companions. We took with us two cart-loads of Scriptures — Gospels, New Testaments, and Bibles — and tracts, chiefly in the Telugu language, but with a smaller supply in each of the five languages we would meet, and which could be used by some of our party, for each one of us could preach in two or three.

We had already been out two and a half months. My sturdy Saugur pony had carried me seven hundred miles, and we had thus far distributed, chiefly by sales, seven thousand Scriptures and books.

Of the dangers promised us we had experienced some. In one city, indeed, we had seen the mob, angry because we preached another God than theirs, swing to the iron gates, shutting us within, and tear up the paving-stones to stone us with; but, by an artifice obtaining permission to tell them just one story before they should begin the stoning, I told the story of the cross in the graphic language that the Master Himself gave me that day, and the mob became an absorbed audience, down the cheeks of many a member of which I saw the tears trickle, as I pictured Christ upon the cross, in agony for us, that we all might be freed from sin. The stones were thrown into the gutter, and when I had done they bought and paid for many Gospels and tracts to tell them more of that wonderful God-man of whom they then first heard.

We had been washed away by a flood, my pony and I being whelmed under by a tropical torrent that rolled swiftly down a river ordinarily fordable as we were in the middle of it crossing; but we had all succeeded in swimming to the same bank.

We had been kept awake through the night more than once by the roaring of the man-eating tigers around our camp in the jungle, as we heaped wood and brush upon our camp-fires all night long, lest in the morning there should be no one left to tell the tale. We had passed through a jungle where three men had been carried off by tigers from the same cart-track in broad daylight just a few days before; but the "I will be with you always" had all the way forefended us from harm.

We had now, however, come to the greatest strait in our journey. We had reached our farthest northern point, up among the mountain Gonds, or Khonds, who for centuries had offered human sacrifices; and after telling them of the one and all-sufficient sacrifice for sin by Jesus Christ, we had turned to the east and south on our return journey by another route. We were to find a government steamer when we struck the Pranhita River, an affluent of the great Godávery. The government was then endeavoring to open up those rivers to navigation, and had succeeded in placing one steamer on the river above the second cataract, to run up to the third. The government officers in charge of the works, having heard months before of my proposed journey, had offered to send that steamer up to the third cataract on any date I would name if I would but take the journey and transport myself and party rapidly through that stretch of fever jungle, which was deadly at this season of the year. I had named the date and received assurances that we could depend on the steamer being there. The heavy torrents of the monsoon had come on unexpectedly early and were unprecedentedly severe. The Godávery became three miles wide of tumultuous waters. Village after village on its shores was swept away. We watched on the banks for a week. A messenger then succeeded in getting through to tell us that the steamer, in attempting to stem that fierce current to come to us, had broken its machinery and could not get to us. We must then march through that seventy-five miles of doomed jungle to reach the next steamer, which was to meet us at the foot of the second cataract and take us down to the first, whence another would take us on.

The government commissioner of the central provinces at Sironcha (for the north bank of the Godávery is under British rule) kindly came to our relief, and, detaching thirty-six coolies from the government works, ordered them, with an armed guard to keep them from deserting, to convey our tents, baggage, medicine chests, and remaining books down to the foot of the second cataract, and we started on.

I need not stop to recount the exciting episode of our desertion, on the north bank of the Godávery, with no human habitation anywhere near, by the whole party of coolies, armed guard and all, nor of our desperate efforts, finally successful, to cross the Godávery's three miles' flood in order that we might reach a large town of the Nizam's dominions, the headquarters of a high native official, a sort of deputy governor, of whom I hoped to obtain help.

Forcing my wiry pony through the three miles of flooded marsh that lay between the river and the town, I appeared at the door of this magnate and politely presented my appeal to him for coolies to take my party down his side of the river to the second cataract. He as politely told me it was an utter impossibility; that at this season of the year, with the fever so deadly and the man-eating tigers so ravenous,—now that the herdsmen had taken their flocks and herds away to the healthier highlands over the fever season, so that they had no flocks to prey upon,—and the floods and back-waters from the river damming the way, no coolies could be induced to go through.

I told him that I must in some way get down to the second cataract, that the steamer that was to come for us had broken down, and that I must have the coolies. I took from my pocket and slowly unrolled a long parchment paper document, a *hookam*, or firman, from the Nizam, which the British minister at that court had kindly pressed upon me as I had tarried a few days at the capital of the kingdom in passing, saying that, though I had not asked for it, he would sleep better if he knew I had it in my possession, for I knew not what I would pass through, nor how much I might need it. I had not thus far opened it.

The need had now come. In it the Nizam, at the request of the British minister, had not only authorized my journey, but ordered any of his officials, of whatever rank, to render any assistance I should call for, either in the way of protection, transportation, or supplies, at the shortest notice and under the highest penalties for nonperformance. The moment the deputy governor saw the great royal seal his whole appearance changed, and, shouting in imperious tones to his belted and armed attendants, he ordered them to run with all speed, each to one of the surrounding villages, and bring in, by force if necessary, the quota of bearers which each village was bound to furnish for a royal progress or for a journey thus authorized.

I had called for forty-four stalwart men, for I felt sure that more than my original thirty-six would be needed before we reached the next steamer. In an incredibly short time the forty-four bearers appeared; they went at once down to the river and brought up all our goods, and with them came the native preachers. They placed the goods in front of the magnate's house.

I made a harangue to them as they stood in a row, each man by his burden, telling them I was sorry to be obliged to compel them to go through the jungle at such a time, or to go ourselves, but we must go; that, to show them that I meant to treat them well, I should now give each one in advance as much hire as he had ever received for going through to the cataract, and that on reaching there I should pay each one twice as much more, in view of the extra risk they ran.

Asking the magistrate what the highest pay was, I placed that sum, in the Nizam's coinage, in the hands of each man, with the magistrate as witness; and when each of the forty-four had grasped it in his palm I told them that now they were sealed to accompany me through; that anyone who attempted to desert me would bring the consequences on his own head; that I had been trifled with the day before, and deserted by those north-shore coolies, who had had no "sealing money," as they call an advance in pay; that I would not be trifled with again; and took out my long navy revolver from my belt and examined its loading, leaving them to draw their own inferences. The magistrate also harangued them, and told them that, traveling under such authorization as this gentleman had, they would be publicly whipped and put in prison if they appeared back at their homes without a line from me that they had taken me through.

To make still more sure, I had separated them into four squads of eleven men each, ordering each squad to march in a compact body, and placing one of the native preachers in charge of each party, to march with them and watch them and give me instant signal if any one put down his burden except at my command. The two royal guides of the region had been ordered to guide us through, and, promised a high reward, had sworn faithfulness.

We struck into the jungle. We had to go single file. Footpaths there had been, but now choked and grown over from the long rains. The second senior native preacher went with the first eleven, the senior preacher at the rear of the last party. The pouring rain would drench us for a half-hour, and then the sun, blazing forth between the sundered clouds, would broil us. The country was flooded and reeking; the bushes were loaded and dripping. Get through we must, or the steamer at the second cataract might not wait for us, and we would then have to march through another lever stretch.

In spite of all my precautions, I felt very suspicious that an effort would be made to desert us before we came to the worst point, and was on the constant watch. Cantering by the whole line where the width of the path allowed, I would stop at the front and watch, and count every man and bundle until all had passed, and then canter on ahead, scanning each man as I went, and halt again. So we went on hour by hour, halting only an hour for lunch at midday.

About 4 p.m. I fancied I saw an uneasiness among the coolies, and rode back and forth more constantly. Three bands had passed me, the fourth was filing by. There was a sharp bend in the path; the last two coolies had not appeared. Quick as thought, striking spur, I dashed across the hypotenuse of the triangle, and jumped my little pony over the bushes into the edge of the path again just as the two coolies had put down their burdens and were springing into the jungle. "What are you doing?" said I, with the muzzle of my pistol at one man's ear. Trembling as though I had dropped from the clouds, they seized their burdens and ran on, overtaking the others. Following, and dashing up the cavalcade to see if all was right ahead, I stopped and dismounted, and appeared to be tightening my saddle-girths, purposely to allow those two men to report to the others what had taken place.

They did report, and word was passed along the line to look out how they attempted to desert, for that they two had tried it when the white foreigner, the *dhora*, was nowhere near, and as they sprang into the bushes the dhora dropped down from the clouds between them, horseback, with his six-eyed gun in his hand, cocked, and it was a wonder their brains were not scattered. And from the way they all looked at me as I rode by again, with my pistol in hand, I knew that superstition was now my ally. They did not know that I would not shoot a man, and my "six-eyed gun" and my mysterious appearance as reported had more terror for them just then than the as yet unseen tigers in the jungle. And on we marched.

But now a new and seemingly insurmountable difficulty confronted us. The dank jungle, the rain, the fever, the tigers, had been taken into account, but in spite of them we had determined to push through and reach the second cataract before the Sunday. But difficulties breed. We now met two fleet-footed, daring huntsmen, who had been down to a point two miles beyond to inspect their traps, and were on the full run back to shelter for the night. Swift and sure of foot, with no impediment, they could before dark make the last village we had passed as we entered the jungle in the morning.

We halted them to inquire about the region ahead. We knew that some two miles in front was an affluent of the Godávery, which ran down from the bluffs at our right, and which we had expected to ford and pitch our camp for the night on an open knoll a little distance beyond it, where, with bright camp-fires and watchfulness, we could pass the night in comparative safety. But from these hunters we learned that the backwater of the Godávery flood, which was thirty feet higher than usual, had made these affluents absolutely unfordable.

"Was there no boat?"

"None."

"No material for a raft?"

"None whatever."

And on the hunters dashed for safety. The two royal guides and I had called them apart alone and questioned them. The guides knew the country well, but this unprecedentedly high back-water was entirely unexpected, and they seemed dazed by the news. The party kept plodding on. We were marching about a mile from the southern bank of the Godávery and parallel with it; two miles farther south were the high bluffs, but with dense, impenetrable, thorny rattan jungle between us and them. The country between river and bluff was flat and flooded.

We knew of only this knoll beyond this affluent where we could encamp. Ten miles beyond it again was another affluent, but that would be flooded as much as this. Still, could we not in some way get across this one and secure safety for one night?

"Guides, if we press on to this little river, can we not make a raft of some kind and get over before dark?"

"Alas! there are no dry trees," they said; "and these green jungle-trees will sink of themselves in the water, even if there were time to fell them."

"Is there no knoll on this side that we can pitch on?"

"No; from river to bluff it is all like this." We were standing in wet and mud as we talked.

"Keep marching on; I will consider what to do."

I drew back and rode behind the marching column. The native preachers had partly overheard the statement about the affluent being uncrossable. From my countenance as I fell back they gathered that we were in straits; they knew that in an hour it would be sunset; dense clouds even now made it seem growing dark. Already we could hear the occasional fierce, hungry roar of the tigers in the rattan jungle at our right. I said not a word to my assistants, but I spoke to God. As my horse tramped on in the marshy path my heart went up and claimed the promised presence.

"Master, was it not for Thy sake that we came here? Did we not covenant with Thee for the journey through? Have we not faithfully preached Thy name the whole long way? Have we shirked any danger, have we quailed before any foe? Didst Thou not promise, 'I will be with thee'? Now we need Thee; we are in blackest danger for this night. Only

Thou canst save us from this jungle, these tigers, this flood. O Master! Master! show me what to do!"

An answer came, not audible, but distinct as though spoken in my ear by human voice: "Turn to the left, to the Godávery, and you will find rescue."

Riding rapidly forward, I overtook the guides. "How far is it to the Godávery?"

"A good mile."

"Is there no village on its banks?"

"No, none within many miles, and the banks are all overflowed."

"Is there no mound, no rising ground on which we could camp, out of this water?"

"It is all low and flat like this."

I drew apart and prayed again as we still plodded on. Again came the answer, "Turn to the left, to the Godávery, and you will find rescue." Again I called to the guides and questioned them: "Are you sure there is no rising ground by the river where we can pitch, with the river on one side for protection and camp-fires around us on the other, through the night?"

"None whatever."

"Think well; is there no dry timber of which we could make a raft?"

"If there were any it would all be washed away by these floods."

"Is there no boat of any sort on the river? I have authority to seize anything I need."

"None nearer than the cataract."

"How long would it take us to reach the Godávery by the nearest path?"

"Half an hour; but it would be so much time lost, for we would have to come back here again, and cut our way through this jungle to the bluff, and climb that; there is no other way of getting around these two flooded streams that we must pass to reach the cataract."

"How long would it take us to cut our way through to the bluff?"

"At least six hours; it will be dark in an hour."

"What shall we do for to-night?"

"God knows." And they looked the despair they felt.

I drew aside again and prayed as I rode on. "Turn to the left, to the Godávery, and you will find rescue," came the response the third time. It was not audible; none of those near heard it. I cannot explain it, but to me it was as distinct as though spoken by a voice in my ear; it thrilled me. "God's answer to my prayer," said I, "I cannot doubt. I must act, and that instantly."

Hastening forward to the guides at the head of the column," Halt!" said I, in a voice to be heard by all. "Turn sharp to the left. Guides, show us the shortest way to the Godávery. Quick!"

They remonstrated stoutly that it was only labor lost, that we should be in a worse plight there than here, for the river might rise higher and wash us away in the darkness of the night.

"Obey!" said I. "March sharp, or night will come. I am master here and intend to be obeyed. Show the way to the river."

They glanced at the fourteen-inch revolver that I held in my hand ready for any beast that should spring upon us. They suspected that it might be used on something besides a beast, and, one saying to the other, " Come on, we've got to go," started on.

All the party had surrounded me. My native preachers looked up inquiringly at my awed face. "There is rescue at the river," was all I said. How could I say more? Providentially we had just come to where an old path led at right angles to our former course and directly toward the river, and down that path we went. The step of all was quicker than before. "The dhora has heard of some help at the river," I overheard the coolies say to one another. I had heard of help, but what it was I knew not. My anxiety seemed to have gone; there was an intense state of expectancy in its place. Half a mile from the river I spurred forward past the guides; I knew the coolies would not desert me now. There was no place of safety they could reach for the night; they would cling around me for protection.

I cantered out from among the bushes to the bank, keenly observant. There, right under my feet, was a large flatboat tied to a tree at the shore, with two men upon it trying to keep it afloat in the rising and falling current.

"How did this boat get here?" said I.

"Oh, sir, please don't be angry with us," said the boatmen, taking me to be an officer of the British India government, to whom the boat belonged, and thinking I was taking them to task for not keeping the boat at its proper station. "We tried our best to keep the boat from coming here, but, sir, it seemed as though it was possessed. This morning we were on our station on the upper river, caring for the boat as usual, when a huge rolling wave came rushing down the river, and snapped the cables, and swept the boat into the current. We did our utmost to get it back to that bank of the river, but it would go farther and farther out into the current. The more we pulled for the British bank, the more it would work out toward the Nizam's. We have fought all day to keep it from coming here, but it seemed as though a supernatural power was shoving the boat over, and an hour ago we gave up, and let it float in here, and tied it up for safety to this tree. Don't be angry, sir; as soon as the river goes down or gets smooth we will get the boat back where it belongs. Don't have us punished for letting it come here; we could not help it."

"All right, my men," said I. "I take command of this boat; I have authority to use any government property I require on this journey. I shall use the boat, and reward you well, and give you a letter to your superior that will clear you of all blame."

The boat, a large flatboat with strong railings along both sides and square ends to run upon the shore, had been built by the British military authorities in the troublous times following the mutiny in those regions, and placed on an affluent of the Godávery, higher up on the north bank, to ferry artillery and elephants across in their punitive expeditions, and it was still kept there. These men were paid monthly wages to keep it always ready at its station, in case of sudden need.

Who had ordered that tidal wave in the morning of that day, that had torn the boat from its moorings and driven it so many miles down the river, that had thwarted every endeavor of the frightened boatmen to force it to the north shore, and had brought it to the little cove-like recess just where we would strike the river? Who but He on whose orders we had come; He who had said, " I will be with you;" He who knew beforehand the dire straits in which we would be in that very place, on that very day, that very hour; He who had told us so distinctly, "Turn to the left, to the Godávery, and you will find rescue"? I bowed my head, and in amazed reverence I thanked my God for this signal answer to our pleading prayer.

The guides now came in sight through the bushes, with all the party following, and looked dazed as they saw me quietly arranging to put our whole party on the boat for the night; and I heard some say to others, " How did the dhora know of this boat being here, and come right out on to it? None of us knew of it or could have found it."

To my native preachers I simply said, " God heard our prayers, and this is the answer;" for I knew that they had been praying on foot while I was praying on horseback. "Yes," said they, reverently; "He has heard our prayer and delivered us. We will never doubt Him again."

We pitched our *raoti*, or long, low soldiers' tent, upon the boat. It exactly covered it, so that we tied the eaves of the tent to the railings of the boat and made a tight house and a secure abode for the night, and within it the whole party were able to gather with all the baggage. Before dark all hands had gathered a sufficiency of wood and brush to keep a bright camp-fire burning through the night on the shore at the end of the boat. It had not rained for the last hour and a half before we reached the boat, nor did it begin again until we were all safely housed on the boat and the camp-fire well burning, with such large logs well on fire that it burned on with replenishing, in spite of the rain, through the night; and it was well that it did, for the tigers had scented us and were eager for prey.

The tent was large enough for us all if we sat up, but not to lie down in; and I sat watching at the shore end of the boat, pistol in hand, through the night, lest, in spite of the fire, a tiger should try to spring on. We heard their roaring and snarling in the bushes near at hand, and once I fancied I saw the glaring eyes of a royal tiger peering at us between the two nearest bushes. But " He shall give His angels charge over thee, to keep thee in all thy ways," was the thought that kept running through my mind after we had, as we settled down for the night, read the Ninety-first

Psalm in the beautiful Telugu language, and offered up prayers of thanksgiving and praise to the Most High, under the shadow of whose wings we were abiding.

At the dawn of day, taking down our tent, we shoved into the stream and floated down twelve miles, past both affluent streams, that were too high for us to ford, and until the roaring of the cataract warned us that we were just coming into the rapids; and there we moored our boat and left it, that the coolies, after they should have taken us to the foot of the barrier, might come back and in it go up again past those rivers and so reach their home.

Of our twenty miles' farther march around the cataract and rapids, in the alternating blazing sun and drenching rain, when one after another of my native assistants fell under that terrible jungle fever, and each, in a state of unconsciousness, was tied in a blanket to a bamboo, hammock-like, and thus borne onward by the extra coolies that I had provided for just such an emergency; while twice I almost fell from my horse from the power of the blistering sun between the rains, but in answer to prayer received strength to mount again and proceed, myself leading the party; of our reaching the river again, and the coolies' joy at receiving their promised double pay, and bounding off for the boat and home; of the smoke of the coming steamer at last appearing, after we had been waiting in that fever bed for a week; of it and another carrying us down two hundred miles of river into open land and inhabited towns again; of our farther journey southward, and all reaching home two months later, restored, guarded, guided, and brought there in safety by the "I am with you always," I must not now write.

I have tried to give a vivid picture of the events of that pivotal day, but nothing can equal the vivid consciousness we had that day of the presence of the Master; nothing can surpass the vividness of the certitude that God did intervene and save us.

Some who have not tested it may sneer and doubt; *but we five know that God hears prayer.*

II. The Man With the Wonderful Books.

ARE you the man with the wonderful books, and have you any more of them?"

The question was put to me by half a dozen men, on an open plain near a village in the northern part of the native kingdom of Hyderabad, in India. I had ridden on in advance of my party to seek for a good halting-place. These men had evidently seen me as I came horseback across the plain, fending off the scorching sun with a double umbrella, and had come out from the village to meet me.

"Brothers," I had said, as we passed the polite salutations of the Telugu country, " brothers, can you point me to some shade-trees near your village, under which I can pitch my tent? The day is hot, and I am weary with a long march."

Without answering my question, scarcely seeming to notice that I had asked one, they looked up at me as I sat on my horse, and eagerly asked, "Sir, are you the man with the wonderful books, and have you any more of them?"

"What books do you mean?" said I.

"Why, one of our townsmen was down at Santatópe last week, Wednesday, at the fair; and there was a foreign gentleman there with books telling about a new religion, and talking to the people. Our townsman did not see the foreigner and did not hear what he said, but he found some of his assistants selling the books in the market, and bought three of them and brought them home; and there has been nothing done in this village since but read those books and talk about them. Are you the man that had them, and have you any more?"

I had been at Santatópe the preceding week at the fair, for I was out on the long exploring and evangelistic tour of more than twelve hundred miles in the Telugu country spoken of in the last chapter, and was now in regions where, as far as 1 could learn, no missionary had up to that time (1863) ever been, and where the name of Jesus had never been spoken or heard. In many of the villages mine was the first white face they had ever seen. It was about a month before the incident "in the tiger jungle."

On the preceding Wednesday we had made a long march, preaching in every town and village and hamlet we came to, from sunrise to eleven o'clock, later than we usually journeyed in that heat, as we had heard of this periodical market, at which buyers and sellers from a hundred towns would be present, and we wished to deliver our message in the hearing of people from as many different villages as possible, and sell them our Scriptures and tracts to carry back in their bundles and baskets, to read each to the people in his own village, that the " seeds of the kingdom" might be scattered far and wide.

Going, as soon as we had rested a little and had had our midday meal, into the fair, which there was held in the streets of the town and an adjoining grove, myself and two of my four native assistants had alternately preached to different audiences all the afternoon. As we entered a street we would mount an old cart or a pile of building materials, — anything that would raise us so that we could be seen and heard, — and sing one of the beautiful Telugu tunes to Christian words, and gather an audience, and then read to them from one of the Gospels, and preach to them of Jesus

Christ and of the full salvation He had wrought out for all the world. Then, selling as many Scriptures, Gospels, and tracts as we could to them for a small price, we would go around into another street or to a lane in the grove, gather another company, preach again, and sell more books, until night had fallen upon us. Meantime the two other native assistants were moving through the crowds of the market, selling books and tracts to all who would buy. We had disposed of many scores of books and tracts, and at last, when the fair was over, had returned to our camp too weary to sleep, but glad to have sent the "message" into a hundred different and scattered towns.

During the intervening week we had been slowly traveling on, stopping to preach in all the villages we passed, and as I rode along on my pony from village to village, often very weary, I had again and again thought of the scenes of that market-day, and wondered if the books carried into the far-off villages, without the voice of the living preacher to explain and enforce them, had been read, and if read understood, and if understood believed; and I confess that my faith had not been as strong as I had wished. Now there was a chance to test the matter.

Without replying to their question as to whether I was the man and whether I had any more books, I asked, "What were those books and what did they tell about?"

"One of them was *Lúka Suvárta* [the "Gospel of Luke"], and another was *Nistáraratnákara* [the "Jewel Mine of Salvation"], and the other was *Gnánabódha* ["Spiritual Teaching"]," they said. The last, " Spiritual Teaching," is a tract of the size of a Gospel, in which the insufficiency of Hinduism to save a soul, and the all-sufficiency of Christianity, are clearly set forth. The " Jewel Mine of Salvation," or the "Gospel in Song," gives the whole plan of salvation in

Telugu poetry, set to their own choicest native tunes. Both these were prepared by the Rev. Dr. H. M. Scudder, and published in the Telugu language by the American Tract Society.

"But what did those books tell about?" I asked.

"Those books," said they, "those wonderful books, say that there is but one God. We thought there were three hundred and thirty millions of gods, but those books say there is but one, and that He is a God of love, and that when He saw that we were sunken in sin, — ah, don't we know that we are! — and that we could not save ourselves nor get rid of our own sins, — have we not tried it and don't we know we cannot? — that then He determined to undertake the task for us, and that — those books say it — He actually sent His own Son into the world as a divine Redeemer, and that He, *Yêsu Kristu* [Jesus Christ], really came here and was born of a woman, like one of us, and that when He had taught the way of holiness by His words and by His example, and had done many marvelous deeds to prove that He really was divine, He actually gave up His own life and let Himself be killed as a sacrifice for our sins; and that He was buried, and after three days He came to life, — those books say so, — and when hundreds of people had seen Him alive He actually went up again into heaven, and that He is there now alive; and that if we pray to Him He will hear us; and that all that we have to do is to repent of our sins, and leave them off, and pray to Him and say, 'O *Yêsu Kristu*, do Thou free me from my sin, and make me Thy child, and when I die take me to be with Thee;' and that He will do all the rest — those books say so; and that when we die we shall go to heaven and be with Him forever. Sir, are you the man that had those books, and are they true, and have you any more of them?"

Who can conceive my joy as I sat there on my pony and heard those men tell what they had themselves already learned from "those wonderful books"? I forgot the toils and dangers of the journey; I forgot then about the mob that had surrounded us in a walled town only a fortnight before, and torn up the paving-stones to stone us with, because we had dared to come among them preaching another religion than theirs. For my thoughts reverted to the fair at Santatópe, and the men from a hundred villages that had taken these books home with them, and I thanked my God that I was a missionary, that He had led me to come forth on this long and difficult journey, that He had led His people to print these books, and sent His Spirit with them when circulated, and that He had rebuked my lack of faith and showed me what the books and His enlightening Spirit could do.

I turned to my impatient questioners and said, "Yes, brothers; I am the man that had those books, and I have a whole cart-load of books like them. Don't you see the cart coming yonder? Please show me a shady place where we may pitch our tents, and you shall have as many books as you want; for we shall stay here until to-morrow morning."

Meantime several of the village watchmen had come up, seeing me talking with the head men of the village, as these proved to be, and, not stopping to answer my question about shade, they turned to these watchmen and said:

"Here, you, Gópal, run to the village of Kistnagar, and you, Málappa, run to Kotta Kóta, and you, Sítadu, run to Gollapalle, and you here, and you there, and tell them all that the man with the wonderful books has come and that he has a cartload more for sale; and tell them to come in and bring their money, and they can get all they want and talk with him, too, about the books. Tell them to come quick, as he is going to be here only to-day, and they may never have another chance."

Ere I had reached the grove to which they took me I saw the men running through the mountain passes to villages three, five, and seven miles away, to tell them to come in and get the wonderful books, and hear the wonderful news of the divine Redeemer, who could take away all our sins.

Before we had taken our breakfast — for we had taken only a cup of coffee on starting at four o'clock in the morning — and were rested enough to begin to talk — for we had already preached in a number of different villages that morning — deputations from the different villages to which news had been sent began to arrive, ready to hear the news and buy the books. They kept us talking from two o'clock in the afternoon until ten o'clock at night. For by the time we had told the story of stories to one group, another group from another village, a little farther away, would have come; and when we went to tell the story over again to them, the first group would not go away, for they said it was so good they wanted to hear it over again.

The crowd around us kept increasing as we took turns in talking and resting, giving each time the story, but each time adding new incidents in the life of the God-man, and new phases of redeeming love, until at ten o'clock we told them that we must lie down and rest now, as we were to start on early in the morning, and they then reluctantly withdrew.

As we lay on our camp-cots we saw throughout the night, whenever we opened our eyes, strange lights flickering in the streets of the town near by, and at daylight, as we rose to go on our journey, they came out from the town with the different books in their hands, with the leaves turned down here and there; for they said they had been reading the books all night, so as to see whether they understood them before we left, for they never expected to find any one else to explain the books after we had gone. How eagerly they listened as I answered the questions they asked from the turned-down leaves! for they wanted to be sure they knew how to obtain this salvation.

I do not give this as a sample of what usually occurs on our preaching tours. God does not often lift the veil; He bids us walk by faith, not by sight. We often meet with opposition or, worse still, with indifference. We often wail with Isaiah, " Lord, who hath believed our report, and to whom is the arm of the Lord revealed?" But now and then God sees fit to raise one corner of the veil and let us see what may occur in scores of scattered villages, of which we shall for the first time learn when we meet those redeemed ones in the land where all is known.

Meantime this one incident in my own experience many years ago is my answer to those who ask, "What is the use of scattering books and tracts in heathen lands without the living missionary to explain them?" God has said, " My Word shall not return unto Me void, but it shall accomplish that which I please." And He fulfills His promise.

III. Encounter with a Ten-foot Serpent and its Results.

THE week following the incident of "the man with the wonderful books," described in the last chapter, occurred an incident which at first threatened to be damaging, but which proved helpful.

We were now in the great teak-wood forest, with trees towering one hundred and fifty feet above the woodman's path, up which we were wending our way to the great Godávery River, and along which path or rough cart-track were clearings every few miles, and villages and cultivation. We had that morning taken a long march, preaching and disposing of Gospels and tracts in every village and hamlet that we passed. At ten o'clock, learning from our guide that about a mile ahead was a large village or town, I rode on in advance to find a place in which to pitch our tent.

As I came near I saw the elders of the city coming out of the city gates — for it was an old walled town — to meet me. Passing the salutations of the day, I asked them where there was a shady place where I could pitch my tent for the day and night.

"You need not pitch your tent," they replied; "here is a new thatched building just erected for a shelter for our cattle. That will be fully as comfortable as your tent and will save the trouble of pitching; please accept the use of that."

Close by us, just outside the gates of the town, was this new building, with roof and walls made of palm-leaves, and with an open doorway, but no door. The floor was the virgin sod, still green, for it had not been used.

I accepted their hospitality, and as soon as my cart came up I took out my camp-cot, and put it in the middle of the hut, and threw myself down to rest while my servant was preparing my breakfast. My native assistants had not yet come up, as they had found another little hamlet after I left them, and had stopped to preach in that.

I was lying on my back on my cot, reading my Greek Testament, which had been my daily companion from a boy. I was holding it up over me, reading a little, and shutting my eyes and thinking a little. This continued for near half an hour. At length the passage I was reading was finished, and I let the arm that was holding the book fall.

Then, and not until then, did I become aware that a huge serpent was coiled around one of the bamboo rafters, with some four feet of his body hanging down directly over my head, with his eyes flashing and his tongue darting out, just above where my book had been and had concealed him. He had evidently been asleep in the roof; the putting in of my cot had awakened him. While I was reading he had let down one third of his body or more, and was looking to see what this leprous-looking white man was about, for he had probably never seen a white man before.

His darting tongue was almost within arm's length of my face when I caught sight of him. I remembered that during my course at the medical college, in the skylight dissecting-room of the old College of Physicians and Surgeons in New York, I once looked attentively over the muscles of the human frame, and wondered whether a person lying down could jump horizontally without first erecting himself. I found it could be done with proper incentives, for off that cot I came

at one bound to my feet without first raising my head, for
that serpent was too near it.

Running to the door, I seized an iron spit some five or
six feet long, with a sharp point, used for roasting purposes
in the jungle, and which was in the cart. Coming back and
using that as a spear, I was successful at the first thrust in
piercing the body of the serpent where it was coiled around
the rafter.

But then I found myself in another difficulty. I caught
hold of the spear to keep it from falling out and releasing
the serpent, but the serpent would draw back, and with
a tremendous hiss strike at my hand that held the spear,
and come suspiciously near hitting it with his tremendous
extended fangs. If I should let go, the spit would fall out and
the serpent would get away, and he and I could not sleep
in that hut together that night, especially after he had been
wounded by me. If I held on, his body might slide down the
spit until he could reach my hand, which might be fatal to
me instead of to him.

However, in answer to my lusty calls, my servant soon
appeared with a bamboo club. Holding the spit with my
left hand and taking the club in my right, I administered
to the serpent a headache, from which he died. As I took
him down and held him up by the middle, on the spit, to
the level of my shoulder, both head and tail touched the
floor, showing that he was about ten feet long.

Just as I was holding him in this position one of the
village watchmen passed the door of the hut going into
the village, and saw what I had done. It occurred to me
at once, that now I should find myself in a " bad box," for
the people revere serpents as demigods. They dare not kill
them or harm them, and will always beg for the life of a
serpent if they see any one else killing one. They think that

if you harm one of these deadly serpents it or its kin will wage war on you and your kin and descendants until your kin are exterminated. I, a missionary, had come there to preach; how would they hear me when I had killed one of their gods?

Knowing that the news had gone into the town to the elders, I began to prepare my line of defense, for I thought that they would soon come out to call me to account. I remembered a verse of one of their Telugu poets commending the killing of venomous reptiles, and having a copy of that poet with me, I opened my book-box and took it out, but had not found the verse when I saw the chief men of the place coming out toward the hut.

To my astonishment, they had native brass trays in their hands, with sweetmeats, cocoanuts, limes, and burning incense-sticks on them; and as they came to the door of the hut they prostrated themselves before me, and then presented these offerings; for they said I had rid them of their most dangerous enemy, that that serpent had been the bane of that village for several years. It had bitten and killed some of their kine and, I think, also a child. They had made every effort to drive it away from the village by burning straw closer and closer to it to make it go farther and farther away, but it would always return. They had tried to coax it away by putting little cups, each holding half a teaspoonful of milk, every two yards or so out into the jungle; but as soon as it had drunk all the milk it wanted it would turn round and crawl back into the village and into some house, and then the people of that house would have to vacate until it chose to leave. It had become the terror of the village.

But now I, a stranger and foreigner, had killed it without their knowledge or consent. That was their safety; for if they had seen me doing it they would have begged for its life, lest they be taken as accomplices. Now it was dead, and they were guiltless, and it could harm them and theirs no more. Would I please accept these sweets? They had sent to the flock in the fields to have a fat sheep brought me as an offering, and would I please accept the sheep? Now whatever I had to say they would listen to me gladly, for was not I their deliverer? The sheep was brought; myself, associates, and attendants made a sumptuous dinner from it. The serpent was not a cobra, — cobras never grow so large, — but it was said to be equally venomous.

When the heat of the day was over we all went into the town to preach. At the gate was the village crier with his tom-tom, or small drum; and as soon as we appeared he went through all the streets beating the tom-tom and crying, "Come, all ye people; come and hear what the serpent-destroyer has to say to us." A royal audience we had, while we spoke to them of the " old serpent " and his deeds, and Christ, who bruised the serpent's head. The killing of the serpent, instead of proving a bar, had opened a door of access to the gospel.

A Noted Banyan Tree.

IV. THE GOSPEL RIVER IN INDIA: HOW IT FLOWS.

We have in India a magnificent river, the sacred Godávery, which, rising on the western coast, only a few miles from the Sea of Arabia, among the hills to the north of Bombay, flows diagonally across the entire country to the southeast, and discharges its waters into the Bay of Bengal, north of Madras.

The monsoon, or rainy season, on the western coast is different from that on the eastern, so that the river comes freighted with its mighty life-giving current during our dry season, flowing with swollen stream through a region parched and verdureless. Some thirty years ago the government of India, incited thereto by an enthusiastic and dauntless English engineer who had on military duty traversed the country, constructed an annicut, or dam, over two miles in length, costing four millions of dollars, across this mighty river, thirty miles from the sea, raising the level of its current some thirty feet, and, digging channels great and small, poured out its vivifying waters over a million acres of what had been an arid plain.

Behold the change. What had for centuries been worthless sand-plains were converted into fruitful rice-fields; the squalid inhabitants have become thrifty farmers; the famine-stricken region is a garden of plenty. What has wrought this marvel in these now harvest-laden counties? It is but the flowing in of the waters of that historic river.

British skill did not create the waters of the Godávery. For centuries it had flowed as now. Bubbling up from springs among the Maráthi Hills, it runs a tiny brook; other springs from hillside and dale feed it as it speeds along; affluents from Berár, Nagpóre, Hyderabad, Bustár, increase its volume; it becomes a river. I have followed its banks or traveled on its bosom for hundreds of miles. It is here a rapid torrent; it is there a placid stream; it is yonder a leaping cataract; here it broadens into a lake; there it foams between the perpendicular walls of a mountain gorge, as it bursts through the Eastern Gháts, whence in a broad and even stream it flows through sixty miles of rolling country and of plain until it buries itself in the sea. It is ever flowing, pure, refreshing, life-giving.

On its banks successive generations had been living for ages and had seen its everlasting flood; successive generations had eked out a squalid existence on the sand-plains a hundred miles southward; but neither had they comprehended its possibilities for good nor attempted to utilize its wasted waters. It was left for a Christian nation, educated by the Bible, brought by the Bible and the Bible's Author to their present proud position among the nations of the earth — it was left for such a nation to discover the possibilities, to advance the capital, to furnish the skill, to turn the watercourses upon the desert, and, while reaping their portion of the gladsome harvest, to confer life, as it were, upon the inhabitants of the droughty plains.

That river is a type, those fruitful gardens an illustration. God's Word, the divine revelation of Himself, His works, His purposes to sinful man, is that river. Its fountains were from the Eden showers of grace on undeserving man. The volume of the river was increased by the successive revelations to Enoch, Noah, Abraham, Jacob, Joseph, Moses,

David, and the prophets. A stream flowing on, it passed the narrow barriers of the Jewish walls, and with the coming of Jesus of Nazareth, His life, His sacrificial death, it widened out into the blessed " river of salvation," broad, placid, refreshing, life-giving, to all who come under its influence. The missionary, the Bible, the tract societies, are striving to make this stream flow over the arid moral wastes of sin-scorched India and cause it to exchange its spiritual desolation for the fruitful beauty of a garden of the Lord.

When the Godávery annicut was completed, and the main channel that should take the stream down through the counties was well under way, the government sent out messengers to all holders of land to tell them what the water would do for them, what harvests it would produce, and that, at a fixed price, any who wished it could have side-channels dug to their own land and avail themselves of the water.

So are the agents of the missionary, the Bible, and the tract societies working in India, sent out with the message, oral and printed, telling the people of the " river of the water of life "; sent out to cry aloud in every market-place, "Ho, every one that thirsteth, come ye to the waters, and he that hath no money; come ye, buy, and eat; yea, come, buy wine and milk without money and without price."

These societies do not create the stream. Like the Godávery, it has been flowing for centuries in rich abundance; but it had not been turned in upon India, and India remained a moral sand-plain, verdureless and fruitless. It was left to foreign Christian nations, to us of this age, aye, in a measure to us of this nation, to introduce those streams to India's teeming millions. It is true that on England, as the conquering nation, fell the heaviest responsibility; and hundreds of her sons and daughters, and thousands of pounds of her wealth, consecrated yearly to the work, show that she is not altogether unmindful of her sacred duty, of her glorious opportunity. But she alone is not equal to the task of converting all India into a garden of the Lord in this generation.

British gold and British skill could dam the river, though two miles broad and with forty feet deep of loose sand lying underneath the flowing water; they could thus change a dozen sterile counties into a fruitful garden. But when Christian England looked upon the moral waste covering all India with her two hundred and eighty-seven millions of Christless inhabitants, it is no wonder that she stood back aghast and eagerly summoned to her aid her willing allies of every Christian nation. And they have come. Germany, Switzerland, Denmark, Canada, and the United States, as well as England, Scotland, Ireland, and Wales, each has her corps of laborers on the field engaged in the hopeless and yet hopeful work.

It is a matter of joy that the myriad Christians of America of different churches, each through its own missionary board and all through the Bible and tract societies, have their share in this work. Let me point out here some of the ways in which we are endeavoring to carry out this work, especially through the aid of printed truth, for the other forms of labor are better known.

The Bible must be translated into the many languages of India, and printed and scattered all through the country; for that is the great channel for conveying the streams of salvation to the people. In this work both of translation and of circulation our own American Bible Society has borne a most admirable part. The Bible has already been translated into eighteen of the chief languages of India, and the New Testament or parts thereof into twenty of the minor languages, and is being circulated by the hundred thousand yearly.

The Bible is the main channel; we must have side-channels and distributing rivulets to bring it within the knowledge and reach of all. Dropping now the figure, let me speak of each of the agencies, aside from the Bible, that we use for bringing the news of salvation in printed form before the people of every age and class and station.

Wishing to catch the attention of the young while their minds are easily impressed, we commence with the school-book. I have lying before me a first book or primer in the Telugu language. It begins with the alphabet of five hundred and thirty-nine characters, and goes on to syllables and easy sentences. Among the easy sentences are these: "There is but one God." In that sentence the foundation of the Hindu system is undermined. "God is a Spirit; He has no body, no visible form." Idolatry receives a stab; for how can an image represent Him that is without visible form? "God is holy; in Him there is no sin." If this is received by the young minds as true, the legends of their impure gods are swept away. "God is love." This is a new conception to the Hindu mind. They fear, they dread, their gods; they make offerings to them to avert their wrath; but they have no thought of God as a loving Father. "God so loved us that He sent His own Son to save us." Here the young Hindu receives his first idea of a loving God reaching down to save sinful man.

Thus, mingled in with other matter, come these germs of saving truth; and on the back cover is printed in large type the Lord's Prayer, that all may learn it; and many not yet Christians love to use it. These first books are sold at from one to two cents each, and so much better are they prepared and printed than the native first books, and so much cheaper, that hundreds of heathen schoolmasters introduce them into their schools in spite of their Christian teaching. On one occasion I sold thirty-five copies to a single heathen schoolmaster to supply his younger pupils. Eighty thousand copies of this one little book, in the Telugu language alone, have already been sold, and probably twice that number in all the languages of India together. These primers are followed by Christian first readers and second readers and other school-books, all pervaded with Christian truth — all sold for cost, or less, to non-Christians who will buy.

Story-books, too, by the hundred are issued; little stories that will take among boys and girls, that will be read for the story, but each one having some Christian truth or moral precept inculcated in it, some with pictures and some without. The smallest are four inches long and two and a half broad, with about sixteen or twenty pages, and with colored paper covers. They are sold for one pie each. The pie is their smallest coin and is worth a quarter of a cent, so that every boy and girl can purchase a little truth-bearing storybook. Of these hundreds of thousands are sold every year among heathen children, and their influence for good is seen in after years in many a life.

V. THE GOSPEL RIVER IN INDIA: THE "GOSPEL IN SONG."

I COME now to speak of the use of the "Gospel in Song." The Hindus, especially the Telugu people, among whom I have worked so many years, are very fond of poetry and of music. All their ancient literature is in poetic form; their grammar and geography, their arithmetic and astronomy, their works on medicine and science and law that have come down from former ages, are in poetry, which they always intone or chant when they read it. Besides this they have sweet and melodious tunes that have come down from great antiquity, and of these they are very fond. Of these old tunes we make use as a vehicle for the gospel. They have, indeed, been sung to the praises of their false gods, often to libidinous words that no respectable man or woman would listen to in public without a blush; but in the desperate conflict that is going on between the powers of darkness and the powers of light in India, wishing to seize the devil's choicest weapons to thrust him with, we take these old native tunes and convert them by marrying them to Christian words, and again send them coursing through the country; and many, glad to be able to sing the old tunes to words that do not make them blush and which at least teach a correct morality, will join in singing the new words for the sake of the old tunes.

I have before me the *Nistáraratnákara*, or "Gospel in Song," issued many years ago in the Telugu language. In it the whole plan of salvation is clearly set forth in songs set to their most loved native tunes; and many a Hindu who has received this has begun by trying to see how the new words fitted to the old tune, and has sung and sung until he has sung away his prejudices, and has sung the knowledge and the love of God and of His Son, Jesus Christ, into his heart, and has gone on singing of his Jesus, *his* Saviour, and will keep up his singing until, thus brought in, he joins in singing the song of Moses and the Lamb.

Who originated this book we do not know; it was in use in several of the languages of India before it was translated into Telugu; but we do know that in each of the eighteen different languages in which it is issued it has been the means of leading many souls out of the thraldom of Hindu superstition into the liberty of Jesus Christ. There are many other poetical tracts, large and small, issued with the same intent, which are willingly received and widely sung by those who thus gain their first knowledge of Jesus and His salvation.

The Telugus also readily catch up and become very fond of our livelier American tunes, especially those with a chorus or refrain; and we make use of them, for the novelty of the foreign music sometimes rivets their attention. Many years ago I translated into Telugu the children's hymn:

> "Jesus loves me; this I know,
> For the Bible tells me so,"

and taught it to the children of our Telugu day school. It was scarcely a week before, as I was going through the narrow streets of the native town, horseback, I heard singing that sounded natural down a side street. I stopped to listen, cautiously drawing up to the corner, where I could unobserved look down the street and see and hear; and there was a little heathen boy, with heathen men and women standing around him, singing away at the top of his voice:

"Jesus loves me; this I know,
For the Bible tells me so. ...
    Yes, Jesus loves me;
    The Bible tells me so."

And as he completed the verse the question arose, "Sonny, where did you learn that song?"

"Over at the mission school," was the answer.

"Who is that Jesus, and what is the Bible?"

"Oh, the Bible is the book sent from God, they say, to teach us how to get to heaven, and Jesus is the name of the divine Redeemer, that came into the world to save us from our sins; that is what the missionaries say."

"Well, the song is a nice one, anyhow. Come, sing us some more."

And so the little boy went on, a heathen himself, and singing to the heathen about Jesus and His love.

"That is preaching the gospel by proxy," I said to myself, as I turned my pony and rode away, well satisfied to leave my little proxy to tell to his interested audience all he himself knew, and sing to them over and over that sweet song of salvation.

The tune of "Hold the Fort" is one that catches the ear and rings in the memory of men of every clime. Go where you will in foreign lands, it is hummed and whistled by men and played by bands who do not even know the words. This seemed a fitting winged messenger to carry the gospel message to our song-loving Telugus, and I prepared such a message in their language adapted to the tune and sent it forth on its journey.

The first time we used it among the heathen we had gone into the native town to hold a gospel preaching service.

We sang this "gospel message" as a rallying-cry, and as we sang the chorus again and again, at the close of each verse one and another of the audience were heard, at first faintly and tentatively, to join in the chorus, which in the Telugu runs thus:

"Yésu Krístu náku gánu
Pránam icchenu;
Tana yodda nannu pilchen.
Krístu vacchedan."

Rendered into English, the message would run:

"Come, ye people! hear the message
By the Saviour given:
God the Father loves His children,
Wishes them forgiven.

Chorus:

"Jesus Christ, my loving Saviour,
Shed His blood for me;
Now He bids me come unto Him;
Christ, I'll come to Thee.

"God so loved the world of sinners,
Ruined by the fall,
That He sought a way to save them
That might save them all.
Jesus Christ, etc.
"For us all, to die and suffer,

His own Son He gave,
That whoe'er believeth on Him
Might not die, but live.
Jesus Christ, etc.

> "'Come, ye weary, heavy laden,'
> Is my Lord's behest,
> 'All your sins and sorrows leaving,
> Come to Me, and rest.'
> Jesus Christ, etc."

After we had closed the meeting, singing the song again in closing, and were going home, I heard in the stillness of the night air one of our heathen audience singing on his way to his house the refrain, "Krístu vacchedan" ("Christ, I'll come to Thee"), and my prayer went up that that message and that refrain, so readily caught up, might go ringing through the country and lead many a sin-burdened Hindu to sing from his heart, "Christ, I'll come to Thee."

We have a Christian song married to one of the most beautiful of the ancient native melodies, that is known all through the country. Its theme is the insufficiency of human schemes and human help to relieve the burdened soul of sin, and the sufficiency and the love of Christ. Myself and native assistants have sung this song in hundreds, yes, in thousands, of different native towns all up through the Telugu country. It is one of those tunes that linger on the ear and prompt a repetition. The Telugu hymn runs thus, for the refrain always comes first in Telugu music:

Refrain:

"Ní charanamulé nammiti, nammiti;
Ní pádamulé battítí, battítí.

I.

"Dikkíka Nívé tsakkagá rávé?

Mikkilí mrokkudu, mrokkudu, mrokkudu.

II.

"Aihika sukhamu narisiti nitya,
Mahaha drohini, drohini, drohini."

Rendered into the same meter in English, it is as follows:

Refrain:

"Thy refuge, safe and free, would I seek,
   blessed Jesus;
Thy mercy-giving feet would I clasp, blessed Jesus.

I.

"My only help art Thou; wilt Thou not hear me?
For on Thee, bowing low at Thy feet, do I call.
   Thy refuge, etc.

II.

"The fleeting joys of earth have not I tasted?
Traitor I wandered far, far away, far from Thee
   Thy refuge, etc.

III.

"My own works, all so vile, filled with pollution,
I abhor, I renounce. Saviour, turn me not away.
   Thy refuge, etc.

IV.

"My hard and sinful will, my baser passions,
Pluck them out, drive them hence; free me,
   Lord, deliver me.
      Thy refuge, etc.

V.

"My nature so corrupt, canst Thou not change it?
Ease my pain, O my God! Save me, Lord, save me now.
Thy refuge, etc."

I well remember one evening in 1863, as we were out on
a long preaching tour of several months up through a native
kingdom, when we were far beyond where any missionary
had ever been, and where the name of Jesus had never yet
been heard, we went into the compactly built town near
which, in a shady grove, our tent was pitched, to preach of
Jesus and His salvation. The people of the town had seen us
pitch our tent as we had finished our morning journey, and
wondered what we had come for. As the sun was going down
we went into the streets of the town, and finding an open
market-place, we took our stand and sang that song with its
sweet refrain, singing the refrain first, as is always done in
native music. An audience soon came together to hear the
music, and listened with wonder to their old familiar tune
and its new words, with their strange message of a Saviour
from sin. And while we preached of Him who alone was
able to change our corrupt nature, renew our sinful will,
and drive out our baser passions, if we would only seek
His safe and free refuge and with earnest desire clasp His
mercy-giving feet, they listened as though it was sweeter
news than any they had ever heard before. We sang the
song again before we left, and then they purchased many
copies of Gospels and tracts and of the " Gospel in Song,"
and we returned to our tents under the trees, to stay until
sunrise, when we would pass on to other villages. We had
had our supper and our evening worship, and had retired,
and all was still, when through the trees we heard the people
in the village singing over the refrain, " Ní charanamulé
nammiti, nammiti," and then they took up the words of the

song, "My only help art Thou; wilt Thou not hear me?" And on in the night, mingled with my sleep, I was conscious of hearing songs of redeeming love, sung by those Hindus, who had until that day never heard of the Bible, never heard the name of that Jesus of whose love they were now singing.

The "Gospel in Song" — who can tell its power? In giving to the superstition-bound Hindus this facility for and love of music, God has put in our hands one of our keenest weapons. We do well if we use it to its utmost, as we try to do; for I have only hinted at a few of the many ways in which we use it to bring the matchless love of Christ before the sons and daughters of India.

VI. THE GOSPEL RIVER IN INDIA:
THE FLEET-FOOTED TRACT.

Among the agencies for diffusing the waters of this river of life, the next is the all-pervasive tract, that goes wherever the alphabet is known. This is an agency of which we make extensive use. Tracts are issued in every variety of form, on every phase of Christian truth, in all the languages, at all prices and no price, and circulated in every imaginable way.

The leaflet, or single-page tract, is scattered broadcast, printed on a little slip of fancy-colored paper to attract the eye, or on a larger leaf when the subject requires more space, sometimes in prose, sometimes in poetry, some in parable, some in proverb, some in questions, some in brief Bible story, all designed to excite interest and provoke further inquiry, and all sent, like the rain, gratuitously through the towns, the villages, the markets, the fairs.

But are they not misused? Yes, they are very often. Does every clover-seed sprout that is sown upon the field? The leaflet has been used by the bazaar man to wrap up snuff for his customer at the fair; and when the customer in his distant home has unwrapped his snuff, he has read the wrapper, neatly printed in his own language, and reading it and pondering it, he has been led to seek for further light; and through that merchant's misuse of that leaflet his customer has been brought to Jesus.

The tickets which we give the patients at our mission

hospitals and dispensaries are really little leaflet tracts. I have lying before me one in the Telugu language, of which I have myself printed thirty thousand and given them to patients that have come for treatment. It is the size of a gentleman's visiting-card and has two leaves; it is printed on thick, strong paper that will not wear out. On the front page with ornamental border is printed "Madanapalle Free Hospital," with blanks for number, date, and patient's name. By that number he is registered, and his disease, symptoms, and treatment are entered on the book. This ticket is given to the out-patients. Each time one comes for further treatment or for more medicine the patient must show this ticket. They keep them very carefully, often for years, lest perchance they want to come again and need this as an introduction. As the patient is registered and receives his number, he seats himself to await his turn for treatment, and opens his folded ticket to see what directions it contains inside. As this may be the only glimmering of truth that some will have in the villages from which some of these patients come, a hundred miles away, I prepared the most concise statement of Christian truth I could and printed it there. He reads:

"There is but one true God. He created, controls, and preserves all things that exist; He is sinless, but we are filled with sin; He, to take away our sin, sent His own Son, Jesus Christ, into this world as a divine Redeemer. That divine Redeemer, Jesus Christ, gave His life as a propitiatory sacrifice, and now whoever believes on Him and prays to Him will receive remission of sins and eternal life. This is what the true Veda, the Holy Bible, teaches us."

He turns over to the last page and finds a quotation from one of their favorite Telugu poets, who wrote seven centuries ago; for we like, as did Paul, to clench a truth by saying, "One of your own poets has said." He reads in Telugu:

> "The soul defiled with sin, what real worship pays it?
> The pot unclean, the cookery, who eats it?
> The heart impure, though it essays devotion,
> Can Deity receive it? Nay, nay. Be pure, O man."

And we add below this: "To give us this very purity of heart, spoken of by your poet, our divine Redeemer, Jesus Christ, came into this world. Believe in Him."

Fifty miles and more from Madanapalle, as I have been traveling, a man has seen me, run into his house, and quickly come out again, holding out one of these tickets, in some instances several years old, as shown by the date, and claimed acquaintance as a former patient of mine; and that ticket has served as an excellent introduction to my preaching there and then to all the people of his village.

These tickets are read. I met upon the highway one day, as I was traveling twenty miles from home, a Brahman, who stopped me and asked if I were not the missionary doctor from Madanapalle. He said that one of my patients had taken home his ticket to his village eighty miles away, and that he had seen it and read it, and read it again, and now he had come in on foot all that way to ask me more about that" true Veda " and the Jesus Christ set forth in that little ticket. Those tickets pay.

Next to the gratuitous leaflets we have small tracts printed in book form with colored paper cover, and sold for one pie, or a quarter of a cent, or two pies or three pies each. We sell as many as we can instead of giving them away; for if a Hindu pays cash for a thing he thinks more of it, keeps it more carefully, and perhaps will lend it more widely than if he gets it for nothing.

Then there is the series of Bible narratives with full-page

pictures printed in colors. I chance to have lying before me "The History of Joseph" in that form. There are seven full-page illustrations and nine pages of narrative. These are sold for one *anna*, or three cents, each, and are very attractive to the Hindus, who like bright colors; and the Oriental pictures, with the characters in a garb that seems so strange to us, have a homelike look to the Hindus, and make them feel, as they look at these Bible characters, that the Bible is not so very foreign a book, after all; and so these colored picture-tracts help to popularize the truth and make the Hindu more ready to read not only the narratives, but also the teachings, of the Christian's Bible. Brief pictorial lives of Christ are thus published, and seeing that He was not a white Englishman in stiff English costume, but appeared and was arrayed much like themselves, they feel more drawn toward Him, or less repelled.

We have also a series of nicely printed wall pictures of Bible characters, scenes, and incidents. They are on stiff paper, about sixteen by twenty-two inches in size. The pictures are printed in colors in England, the picture covering one half the page, and the lower half left blank; and so they are sent out to Madras, where the Christian Knowledge Society prints on each the story or the explanation in Telugu, Tamil, Kanarese, or Hindustani, and mission presses in other parts of India print the same in the languages of their districts. These, thus printed, are sold at six cents each.

Some years ago I obtained a number of sets of these pictures with the story or the explanation in the different languages read at Madanapalle, and hung them around the walls of our free reading room, with an intimation that copies of any of them could be had for two *annas*, or six cents, each.

It was not long before the colporteur in charge came,

asking me to order another lot, as these had all been sold; and most of the purchasers had been well-to-do non-Christians, who gladly bought them, in spite of their Bible stories, to enliven the walls of their own houses. And many a time, as I went to see some patient in a high-caste Hindu's home, I found some of these pictures on the walls, with the Bible story on them, where all the family could read. The infant Jesus at Bethlehem, the boy Jesus in the temple, talking with the gray-bearded priests, the man Jesus raising the widow's son, the Christ Jesus talking with the woman at the well, all in their richly colored Oriental costume, appealed to their sympathies, attracted their attention, familiarized them with scriptural imagery, and made them the more ready to read the fuller accounts of the same incidents in the " true Veda."

Larger tracts of fifty or more pages are yet sold for one cent each. We always sell at or under cost, for our object is to circulate as broadly as possible. We only obtain price enough to secure good usage for the tract. And are these tracts read? Some are not; some are.

Near forty years ago such a tract, called "Spiritual Teaching," written by Dr. H. M. Scudder, found its way into a Telugu village seventy-five miles northwest of my present station in India. It fell into the hands of one of the head men of the village. He was a high-caste man of noted probity of character. He read it, and then re-read it with more attention. It was the first he had heard of any other religion than Hinduism. He had always longed for some help to get rid of his sin; this opened to him the way to get such help. He read the tract to his wife and little boys, and told them it was so good it must be true. He read it to his neighbors, and some of them also accepted its teachings. At last he heard of a missionary who taught similar doctrines some seventy miles away; he went on foot across the then roadless country, through the hills, to the town where the missionary was said to live. He found him, told him what he had learned from the little book, and asked if it were true and if he knew about the God that had given His own Son to save us from our sins. He went back and brought his family with him to hear more of this wonderful news. They were all baptized by the missionary, and he placed his children in the mission school, there to be educated, that they might help make known these glad tidings to his countrymen. In 1861 I buried the old patriarch in a Christian's grave. He was a man of strong faith and much prayer; he spent his last breath in sending up shouts of praise to his Saviour for sending this tract out to his village and through it saving him from his sins.

Two of his sons have since been laboring under my direction as preachers of the same gospel. The elder was for a long time native preacher of the church at Palmanér. In 1884 I stood by his bed and saw him pass through the pearly gates. So much respected and beloved was he by all that at his funeral, both at his house and at the grave, there was, besides the Christian congregation, a large concourse of heathen and Mohammedans present, and many a tear dropped into his grave with the flower or the handful of earth that each one, Hindu as well as Christian, reverently cast in. After the funeral a prominent Hindu said to me, "Sir, he was a man who never ceased to tell others of his Saviour. When he was sick in your hospital one of my family was also a patient in the same ward, and I was there a great deal. Every day, and often during the day, he would gather groups of the patients and their friends around him, and read to them from his Bible, and talk to them of the love of Jesus Christ and of His willingness to take away the sins of all who would come to Him and ask. Yes, sir, he was a good man, and we Hindus too mourn over his loss."

This was accomplished by that one tract that found its way all alone into that distant Hindu village. Thousands of Hindu souls in glory will point back to the leaflet or the tract that, wafted or borne to their distant homes, first told them of and bade them seek " the river of the water of life."

These are some of the channels through which the " gospel river in India" is flowing and being distributed, in tiny rivulets, to thousands of separate and scattered villages; aye, and in many an unpromising locality are already found germinating seeds and growing fruits, that give promise of developing into a garden of the Lord.

VII. Establishing A New Station: Varieties In Mission Work.

I AM often asked, " How do you proceed in establishing missionary work in a new region? How do you get hold of the people? How do you first introduce Christianity to them? There are no halls to be hired for preaching in, no daily papers in the up-country regions in which to advertise the proclamation of a new doctrine at a given place and hour. The whole mass of the people is either indifferent or hostile to you. How, then, do you gain your first foothold and start the missionary machinery working in new regions? And what are the different kinds of missionary activities?"

I am in a position to answer these questions, for in 1863 I was chosen to go on into new regions and open out work among the Telugu people, the work in the Arcot Mission, with which I was connected, having thus far been almost entirely confined to the Tamil people, adjoining the Telugu border on the south.

With three native assistants, a catechist, a reader, and a school-teacher, all of whom knew Telugu, which I also was able to use freely, we entered our "new diocese."

As Europeans and Americans cannot live and keep their health in the ill-ventilated native houses in the thickly built streets of the India towns, even if the caste Hindus would permit them so to live, and as none of the very few European houses built for the government officials in the outskirts of the town could be had, it was necessary for myself and family to live in a tent while we were erecting a small house. We thus lived through the hottest months of the year, when the butter would sometimes turn into oil upon our dining table, and on through the first burst of the early monsoon, or rainy season, when from the torrents of rain the earthen floor of our tent became so moist that our chairs would sink down to the rounds, and we would find a crop of green mold grown out on our shoes if they stood unused for a day or two, our clothes would feel damp when we put them on in the morning, and all was reeking with moisture around us. When two rooms of our little house were roofed in we moved into them, as preferable to a tent in such weather, especially for our little children, and proceeded to the completion of the house.

As soon as the rain was over we put up a little schoolhouse church with mud walls and thatched with rushes, in which we held our Sabbath services for the very few native Christians who had accompanied us, and any others who might come in, and in which during the week we gathered a few children from the town, together with the children of our native assistants and servants, and opened a day-school.

Out of curiosity a number of the non-Christian townspeople would come to our Sunday services in the little church, to see how we carried on Christian worship and to hear what was the doctrine which we believed and preached.

Meantime our native assistants and myself had been busily engaged in preaching each morning or evening in all the different streets of the town, and in the fifty villages and hamlets within four miles of our house.

For this village preaching we would start early enough in the morning to reach the village in which we were to preach a little before sunrise, so as to gather an audience before the people went to their work for the day. Walking through the main streets and some of the side streets of the always compactly built village, we would select the best place to gather an audience, and mounting a pile of timber or heap of stones, or some partly tumbled-down wall, or some cart left in the street, we would ring our bell for the meeting by singing a Christian lyric to one of their beautiful Telugu tunes. The Telugus, as I have indicated in a preceding chapter, are exceedingly fond of music, and especially of their old weird and sweet tunes, which have come down through perhaps a hundred generations, sung by them, indeed, to the praises of their gods, but melodious and captivating and well suited for vehicles for God's message of love.

Perhaps we would not see a single person stirring when we began to sing, but in the still morning air the voice of song would enter through the barred windows and through the cracks under or above the doors, and many a one, hearing the voice of singing, would spring from the mat on which he had slept, and come out, with the blanket or coarse sheet under which he had slept wrapped around him, to see what was the occasion of this early music. Seeing a party of strangers with a white foreigner standing together and singing, they would often come forward and listen as they were, while others, already dressed, would one after another join the throng, until sometimes we would have one half the village population gathered around us by sunrise, one third of whom would be wrapped in the blankets in which they had slept.

As soon as a good audience had assembled we would cease our singing and read a portion from the Bible, the catechist or reader would explain the passage and preach to them, and the missionary would follow, presenting God's love for man and the scheme of salvation through Jesus

Christ more fully to them. At the conclusion one-page leaflets, containing a statement of Christian truth, would be gratuitously distributed, and Gospels or tracts of larger size would be offered them for a very small price, much less, indeed, than their cost, and which many a one would purchase because they were so cheap, and because they had paid money for them, even though a small sum, would keep them and read them.

While the matter of our message was the same in all the villages,—man in a state of sin and wretchedness, and God's plan for saving lost man, — yet the manner of giving the message would vary according to the degree of intelligence of the audience assembled to hear us. If it were an audience of ignorant laborers, we would in the simplest terms tell them of God our Father, who "so loved the world, that He gave His only begotten Son, that whosoever believeth in Him might not perish, but have everlasting life," and in simplest terms tell them how they could avail themselves of that love and find that salvation.

If it were a village of more cultivated people, especially where there were a good number of Brahmans, we would use higher illustrations and more ornate language, but still give the same message: man in sin, not at peace with holy God, man's utterly hopeless state, and God's way of giving life eternal, with quotations from their poets and their Vedas in illustration of the truth that we presented to them. Such villages we would more often visit in the evening, so that there might be more time for conversation or discussion. We would commence our services a little before sundown, but it would often be late at night before we would reach our home.

Our preaching in the different streets of the town was the same in character, varying in our manner of presentation with the varying culture of the audiences before whom we spoke, whether in the farmers' or the artisans' or the merchants' or the Brahmans' street.

Sometimes we would meet with the most courteous reception, and our message would be listened to with kindly attention, and the questions asked at the conclusion of the preaching would be with the design of further elucidating the bearing of the truths which we had presented before them; sometimes we would be met by stolid indifference or by contemptuous sneers; and sometimes we would encounter angry opposition, and a sharp and long-continued discussion would ensue. It is then that the missionary feels the necessity of claiming the fulfilment of the promise, "I will be with thy mouth, and teach thee what thou shalt say." And God fulfils it often in a wonderful way.

This oral proclamation of the gospel, of God's way of life, in the vernaculars of the people, to the high and the low, the learned and the ignorant, is the chief weapon made use of in the Arcot Mission; for the potency of such proclamation of the gospel, backed by the printed Word freely distributed, is with us a fundamental doctrine.

To obtain more of a hold on the higher classes, it has been the custom of many missions to establish, from the incipiency of a mission, Anglo-vernacular schools of a higher grade, in which instruction is given in all the usual secular subjects, but with a daily Bible lesson, studied by all the classes and expounded by Christian teachers. In our mission, however, such schools have followed the accession of numbers as a necessity for the education of our own young people, and to them non-Christians are admitted and pursue the biblical studies with the Christian students. Such schools have been productive of blessed results.

After the mission has gained a foothold in a region and

more of the young men are being educated, a desire begins to spring up that the girls too should have a chance to learn. Prompting and fostering this desire, we can then open schools for the high-caste Hindu girls, and, visiting them in their homes, we can open out zenana work for educating their older sisters who cannot come out to a school, and often their mothers also and aunts will join those little classes. Our Bible women, too, begin to find access to many houses, and the missionary ladies find their hands more than full in following out these most promising openings. Such work, however, cannot find an entrance usually on the first opening of work in a new region.

In the Arcot Mission the medical missionary work has the rather been our adjuvant in gaining the confidence and affections of the people. When that agency is employed it is essential that two missionaries should be associated in opening the work in a new region; the one to give his almost exclusive attention to direct evangelistic work at headquarters and in all the surrounding region, the other being at liberty to devote himself mainly to his hospital and medical work, always, however, coupling with that work the daily proclamation of the gospel to the multitudes that flock together to receive from him medical or surgical aid.

As I went alone into this new region in the Telugu country, it was designed that I should give my exclusive attention to evangelistic work; and this I did for the first few months, expecting so to continue until joined by another missionary.

But God ordered otherwise. Scarcely were we settled in our new temporary house when the annual drawing of the idol-car in the town occurred. At eleven o'clock at night, as with torch-light procession the car was being drawn by the multitude, it became set; the ropes snapped, but it could not be moved.

"The gods are angry! The gods are angry!" shouted the priests. "Run and bring cocoanuts to break over the wheels and propitiate the gods, or we are lost."

Off ran the people to get cocoanuts for the libation. They were broken on the big wooden wheels, and the milk ran down freely. A well-to-do high-caste farmer had brought his. In striking one on the wheel to break it, it had slipped and fallen on the ground inside the wheel; he reached his hand in under the front of the wheel to get the cocoanut; the people were straining at the mended ropes; just then the "gods became propitious," the car moved forward with a lurch, and passed over the hand and forearm of the farmer reaching for his cocoanut, breaking the bones and mangling the flesh.

From my treatment of some of the workmen who had met with accidents in the building of my house or were taken with cholera, the people had come to know that I was a doctor. His friends carried the wounded man to his house in the main farmers' street of the town, and ran a quarter of a mile to my house to waken me and ask me to come and save the man's life and if possible his arm and hand, the right hand. Taking restoratives and necessary appliances, I hastened to his house to find them singing the death-wail over him. From nervous shock and loss of blood he had fainted, and they supposed him to be dead. The Lord gave me that man's life. How I worked over the case! There were ten bone fractures, besides the mangling of muscles, sinews, nerves, and blood-vessels. How our few Christians prayed! The man recovered and regained the use of even that hand, his plow-hand.

He was a member of a large and influential family connection of landed farmers. Not one of that family ever joined in those idol-car observances again. Few Sabbaths passed that some of them were not seen in our Christian service. None of them openly embraced Christianity, but from that day they were all the Christians' friends and defenders, and a few years later one of them, though not baptized, died calling on the Lord Jesus.

From that time I could not prevent the people coming to me for treatment, especially in surgical cases, where their old-time native doctors were utterly powerless. Little by little was I led to enlarge that department of my work, until, single handed and with only such assistants as I had trained by daily practice, I often had more than one hundred patients in a day in my little mud-walled and thatched-roof dispensary.

This medical work had thus far been generously supported by our English friends, mostly government officials, whom and whose families I was often called to treat, as there was at that time no other surgeon or physician within seventy-five miles.

Now, however, it became necessary to put this work upon a better footing. Government aid was tendered, proper buildings were erected, and in 1869 a well-appointed hospital, as well as dispensary, with qualified assistants, was organized and placed upon a permanent footing, with the medical missionary as its superintendent.

But this distinctively medical work, or rather medico-evangelistic work, which Providence thrust upon me, and to which I was led to give so much of my time and strength for many years, cannot be detailed in this volume, for its magnificent opportunities and its blessed fruits would alone require a volume for their presentation.

Section of Banyan Tree, Showing its Mode of Growth.

VIII. GOSPEL PREACHING TOURS.

WHEN our house was completed and our tents were at liberty we commenced systematic gospel preaching tours through all the villages of our "new diocese."

We would take our tents, with a good supply of Gospels and tracts and some New Testaments and Bibles, chiefly in Telugu, but with always a few in Hindustani, Kanarese, and Tamil, in case we should meet any who knew only one of those languages, and go out for a tour of several weeks.

Our first camp we would make some seven or eight miles from our station in one direction or another, and pitching our tents in a shady grove near some central village, we would preach in each of the villages within a radius of four miles of the tents; and then, moving our tents eight miles farther on, preach in all the villages within a similar circuit, and then move again, so continuing the process as long as we were able to be out.

Each morning while on these tours we would preach in three or four or more villages, and each evening in two or three. Leaving our tents at or before the first break of day, so as to catch the people before they should go out to their fields for their day's work, we would go first to the farthest village in which we expected to preach that day. Reaching that village usually before sunrise, before the people were astir, we would gather them together by the voice of song as we stood in the street; or, if very early, marching through the streets singing to awake the slumberers, we would soon find ourselves surrounded by an audience of curious listeners.

Presenting the truth to them in the way indicated in the last chapter, we would give out a few single-page leaflets, printed on paper of bright colors, of which the Hindus are very fond, and offer Scriptures, Gospels, and tracts on sale at a very small price. Bidding them good-by and inviting them to come and see us at our tent, or at our station whenever they should come to the periodical fair, to learn more about this divine way of life, we would make our way to the next village on our way back to our tent.

There the people had already arisen; the weavers would be getting their looms ready for their day's work, the farmers would be yoking their oxen to go to the fields, the carpenters sharpening their tools for their day's work, and the blacksmiths starting the fire in their forges; but at the voice of the singing they would come together to listen to what these strangers had to say.

When we came to the next village we would find many of the people already at their work, and those who tilled the farther fields would be beyond our reach, and our audience would consist more of children; and the women, standing in their back yards peering over the walls, would listen to our clearly spoken message, while the old men and those who had not yet gone to their work would form no small part of the audience.

At a later hour, when the sun was too hot to allow of our gathering an audience or ourselves preaching in the open streets, we would often find a group gathered on the platform under the village council-tree. Such a tree is found at the entrance of very many of the Hindu villages, large or small. This council-tree is usually a banyan-tree, though sometimes a margosa or a mango or some other tree, and under it is a platform of stones or of sun-dried bricks, covered over with slabs of granite, raised some two feet or more above the level of the street, where the " elders " of the village meet to discuss affairs and settle disputes and administer rural justice. The platform is from twelve to twenty feet square, giving room for a good number of the better class to be seated, Hindu fashion, cross-legged like a tailor, while others stand around or sit on their heels in the street, as we, seated on one edge of the platform, are preaching to them. If we wish to retain our audience we must ourselves sit down, for it is not polite for those being instructed to be seated while their teachers or preachers stand.

If there is no village council-tree, there will usually be found in the main street a council-shed, or *chávadi*, the whole side toward the street being open, and that is a favorite place for us to gather our audience and preach when the sun is too hot for us to stand in the street.

We usually return to our tents by about nine o'clock; at some seasons of the year, however, when there is little work in the fields, we can gather an audience until a later hour. I have myself, accompanied by one native preacher, start-ing before daylight from the tent, made a circuit of eleven miles on foot, preaching in seven villages or hamlets ere returning to my breakfast at my tent at eleven o'clock, and then, the evening being moonlight, we preached in four more, making eleven villages or hamlets in which we two had given the divine message in that one day; and it was the first time that any of these people had heard the name of Jesus. We usually went two and two to the villages, the senior catechist taking the junior assistant, and another assistant accompanying me. We always kept an accurate record of the villages in which we preached, the number of persons who listened to us in each village, male and female, and the number of books or tracts sold or given away.

From each center where we pitched our tent we would reach thirty or fifty or seventy villages, according to the density of the population, before we moved our tent to the next center. Sometimes we would find even more villages than this. I remember pitching our tent in a plain between the hills in 1868, where, by extending our radius to five miles, five of us reached one hundred and sixty villages in eighteen days before we moved our tents.

In one year myself and three native assistants had thus preached in ten hundred and sixty-one different towns, villages, or hamlets, our audiences aggregating twenty thousand and twelve, as we found on going over our records on the 31st of December. We had preached in many of the towns from two to six times each, but at least once had the gospel been proclaimed that year in more than one thousand villages, and this had covered not more than one third of the circuit, with a radius of sixteen miles, around our station.

This shows the density of the population, and indicates how even the agricultural population is all gathered in villages; for none of the farmers live out upon the land which they cultivate. Their flocks and herds also are during most of the year, for safety's sake, brought into the village folds or stables over the night. The people all thus dwelling in villages gives us a far better chance to reach them than though they were scattered all over the country as in America. The hamlets are often quite small, having perhaps not more than fifty inhabitants in some, while many villages of farmers will number a thousand people, and a number of villages in each *táluk*, or county, will number from three thousand to five or even ten thousand people. To every one of these hamlets, villages, or towns do we endeavor, on our tours, to carry the offer of eternal life through Jesus Christ our Lord.

IX. GOSPEL PREACHING AT HINDU FAIRS.

BESIDES these systematic gospel preaching tours in the villages spoken of in the last chapter, we endeavor to reach as many periodical fairs and markets as we can without neglecting other work.

Every táluk has a weekly market at two or more different centers. At each one of these weekly markets or fairs people from fifty to one hundred villages will gather; the farmers bringing in their crops, the weavers their cloth, the fruit-raisers their fruit, the gold- and silversmiths their workmanship, the spice merchants their spices from distant centers, and householders from several hundred families come together to buy their supplies.

The roads and the foot-paths across the fields leading toward the market-places will be alive with travelers from morning until ten o'clock or noon. This weekly market is often held in some large grove. Hundreds of little tents will be pitched, under which the more expensive wares will be exhibited, while the shade of the trees is sufficient for the multitude of those who have less costly wares, or vegetables and fruits. From noon until 3 p.m. the fair is in full blast, and continues, with slowly lessening crowds, until four to six o'clock, when all the people will have departed for their homes.

To visit these markets we have to be out in the heat of the day; but the opportunity is so good to gather large audiences of those who have come from fifty or more villages, and perchance send by them a little seed of truth out to many of these distant places, that we brave the sun and give our day to the one market with its half-score or more of successive audiences. We keep a list of all these weekly or monthly fairs in each of the táluks in which we work, with the dates on which they are successively held, so that whenever we are in a county we may attend any of the fairs within reach of the place where we are encamped.

At some of these fairs we find the people too much engrossed in business to give us much attention; still, by mounting a platform under some tree a little way from the busy bustle of the fair, we can always secure an audience more or less attentive, and who will stop a longer or shorter time to hear what these preachers say. At other times so many of the people attending the fair will leave their business and come to our preaching places, and listen so attentively and so long, as to interfere decidedly with the business of the fair.

I well remember going out to such a weekly fair many years ago, in. the northwest corner of my field. It was the first time that the gospel had been carried there. Reaching the market grove with my two native assistants by two o'clock in the afternoon, we took our stand under a tree on a little rising ground adjacent to a low, flat-roofed temple, which some devotee had erected many years ago at this grove in fulfilment of a vow.

We sang our songs of Zion; a large crowd surrounded us. One of us preached and then another. The crowd increased until not one half of those who had come together to hear us could see or hear the preacher.

One of the interested hearers, who was of short stature and too far away to hear distinctly where he could not see the speaker's face, pressed through the crowd and made a singular suggestion; it was that the missionary should mount upon the flat roof of the temple and speak from there, saying that then all the people at the fair could both see and hear. A murmur of assent through the crowd witnessed their approval of the proposition. By their aid the temple was mounted. The hum of the market ceased, because the buyers and the venders had nearly all of them come forward to listen. The Hindu merry-go-round had ceased its circumvolutions, because the riders of the wooden horses and the people who managed it had all joined the expectant crowd. The Hindu jugglers under an adjacent tree had put their paraphernalia in their sacks, for no one would watch their performance now. The snake-charmers adjacent had covered their serpents in their little flat baskets and, tying the covers on, had mingled in the audience. The *mittai* venders, or sweetmeat merchants, alone remained at their stalls, as the luscious sweetmeats were too great a temptation to the crowd of boys around; but the cloth merchants and the grain merchants and the iron merchants had left their wares without any one to guard them, or at least but one to several stalls, while all the others pressed toward the temple.

In the hush that followed and with the clear-sounding Telugu language, the voice of the missionary could be heard by all the assembled multitude, and he could see every person in the crowd as he stood ten feet above their heads. I was never more impressed by any audience to whom I have ever spoken than by those multitudes, who had deserted their stalls and their traffic and pressed forward in eager silence to listen, for the first time, to that wondrous message.

"Brothers," said the missionary, " I have come from far to tell you the best news that was ever heard by mortal ears. I will tell it to you now, and when I have done I will gladly answer any questions which you may put to me about this wonderful message.

"Brothers, there is but one true God. He created, preserves, and controls all things. We intelligent men could not look up to a God whom we did not acknowledge to be superior to ourselves in every way. He must be wiser, stronger, holier than we, or we could not reverence Him. This true God, that made all worlds, is omnipotent, omniscient, and omnipresent; He sees all things; He sees us here and now. That God is holy, He is without sin; but we are filled with sin; there is not a man among us who dare stand forth and say,' I am without sin.' So long as we are polluted with sin and God is holy there can be no peace, no communion between us sinful men and holy God. This your own poets and sages freely admit and teach. Does not your own Telugu poet, Vémana, say:

'The soul defiled with sin, what real worship pays it?
The pot unclean, the cookery, who eats it?
The heart impure, though it essays devotion,
Can Deity receive it? Nay, nay. Be pure, O man."

"Will desert fastings, or pilgrimages to shrines, or bathing in the holy Ganges, or physical tortures make us at peace with God? Does not Vémana say:

'Tis not by roaming deserts wild, nor gazing at the sky;
'Tis not by bathing in the stream, nor pilgrimage to shrine;
But thine own heart must thou make pure, and then, and
    then alone,
Shalt thou see Him no eye hath kenned, shall thou
    behold thy King.'

"We cannot ourselves by our own effort attain this purity of heart and atone for the sins that we have committed. My

Brahman brothers, whom I see standing before me here, do you not in your evening ablutions at the river chant this Sanskrit *slóka*?

'Pápáham, pápa karmáham, pápátma, pápasambhavaha,
Tráhi mám, Krapayá Dáva, sharana gata vatsala.'

"Does not that mean, 'I am a sinner; my actions are sinful, my soul is sinful; all that pertains to me is polluted with sin. Do Thou, O God, that hast mercy on those who seek Thy refuge, do Thou take away my sin.' You thus roll it back upon God, yourselves not knowing how it can be done.

"Brothers, there is a way by which we can get rid of this burden of sin and of all sin's consequences. It is to tell you how that can be done that I have come here. My ancestors, in the far-away land, used to worship idols and wander in darkness as you do now. Men who had learned of the true God and of His way of expiating sin came and told my ancestors all about it; they accepted the new way; they found pardon, peace, and joy; and my people have sent me here to tell you how you too may find it.

"God, our Father, is a God of love. He 'so loved the world, that He gave His only begotten Son, that whosoever believeth in Him might not perish, but have everlasting life.' He sent His Son into this world to take upon Himself our natures, to become man like us, to show us the way of life, and to expiate our sins. That Son of God, Jesus Christ, was born into this world, of a virgin, as an infant. It was not in the land where we English-speaking people dwell that He was born. Midway between this your land and the land of the English there is another country, Judea, a part of your Asia. He was born there, not as a white man wearing European clothes and speaking the English language; nay, He was born more like yourselves, more of your complexion, wearing Oriental clothing like yourselves, the son of Oriental parents, living amid Oriental surroundings. We of the far West, though so different, have accepted Him as our Saviour, for He is the Saviour of the whole world, and we bring Him to you of the farther Orient as your divine Redeemer."

The missionary then told them of the birth in the manger of Bethlehem, when the wise men of the East brought their gifts; of His spotless life; His marvelous works of healing and mercy; His parables and His teachings; His sacrificial death, when He atoned for the sins of the whole world if they would believe in Him; of His burial, His resurrection, His ascent to the right hand of God; His mediatorial reign there for us; and told them all that they needed to do was to be sorry for and repent of and forsake their sins, and come in faith to Jesus Christ, and say to Him in prayer, "O Jesus Christ, I am a sinner; I cannot get rid of my sin. Thou canst take it away; do Thou take away all my sin and make me Thy disciple, and when I die take me to dwell with Thee;" that if they would do this sincerely and follow that Jesus lovingly, He would do all the rest; that this was the message that we had come from far to bring to them.

For nearly half an hour that whole audience had listened with the closest attention, and when the missionary ceased speaking, earnest questions were asked by the eager listeners, answers to which kept the audience still lingering from their trade; and when the missionary, climbing down from the temple roof, and his assistants offered for sale the " Life of the Divine Redeemer," as the Gospels are called, with tracts that explained the way of salvation more fully, from many a wallet money that had been brought to purchase other things was spent to buy the printed message to carry to their distant homes, to be read by their families, their neighbors, and their friends.

It is not always, by any means, that we are listened to with this eagerness. Often there are angry interruptions made by priests who have perchance come to the fair; sometimes there are discussions which continue for an hour or longer, listened to by from one to five hundred intently to their close. We do not court these discussions in public, as angry passions are likely to be aroused, and an angry man is rarely ever convinced of the truth presented by his opponent. But we do not shun them when brought upon us, for the attention of the listeners is by them sharply drawn to the difference between God's plan of salvation and the best heathen system. And the seed dropped is likely to be carried to many scattered villages by those who have listened without an angry spirit of opposition.

A HINDU VILLAGE.
Counsel Tree and Chevade in Foreground.

X. TREATED WITH A SHOWER OF STONES

THE rapt attention on the first presentation of the gospel message on the part of a Hindu audience, such as detailed in the last chapter, is not by any means the rule in our preaching in the fairs and the streets. A marked case of the opposite kind comes vividly to my mind, and my notes made at the time furnish further details.

While on a tour in the northeastern corner of the Mysore kingdom, which extends to within ten miles of Madanapalle, Catechist John Hill and myself had gone from our camp into a densely populated town. At the cross-streets in front of the village chávadi, or council-house, we had taken our stand, and ere long were surrounded by a goodly number of people, many of whom were Brahmans. They listened to our singing, to our reading from the Scriptures, with scowls and evident hostility, but did not enter into argument. When we had finished we offered them the leaflets, tracts, and Gospels as a gift, but they would have none of them. We could get no kindly response to anything that we said. We turned to go back to our tent.

As we passed slowly down the street a hooting began behind us, and soon small stones, pellets of earth, and other missiles began to shower upon us. One stone the size of an egg struck me on the head, but my pith hat prevented its doing harm. Turning to the catechist who accompanied me,

I said, "We must go back and meet these people. It will not do to let them think that we are driven away from our work."

Turning around, we both walked steadily back toward the hooting and missile-throwing crowd. Seeing our quiet mien and fearlessness, the crowd gave way. Walking directly up to the group of Brahmans in front of the chávadi, to whom we had been chiefly preaching, and who, we believed, were the instigators of this attack, I said to them:

"Brothers, if you wish to stone us, you may stone us to our face. We have come back to you so that you can hit us every time. But first we would like to know why it is that you stone us. Is it because we, leaving our country, have come at our own expense to tell you of what we consider the best news ever revealed to man? Is it because we have told you that the God who made us all so loved the world that He sent His only begotten Son to suffer and die for us, that a way might be opened for the pardon of our sins? Is it because we have told you that the Son of God came to this world, and took upon Himself our nature, and became man in order that He might understand all our weaknesses and temptations and become to us a sympathizing High Priest? Is it because we have told you the divine words of instruction and comfort which He spoke to those about Him and left on record for you and us?"

The whole crowd had by this time pressed forward to listen to what we were quietly saying to the Brahman priests. The priests themselves seemed to feel ashamed of what had been done and were now ready to listen. Point by point, asking them if it was for this or for that that they pelted us, I went over each topic of my previous discourse. All listened eagerly now. The sullen, hostile look had gone. Shame for themselves and evident appreciation of the spirit that we had shown led them ere long to interrupt me, saying, "It was only some of the vagabonds that cast stones at you; we will now see that you have fair play."

When we had finished our second preaching to them, and told them that we had in our hands a history of this divine Redeemer, the Gospel of Luke, which we would sell them for a *duddu*, one of their coins, worth about one cent each, and asked if they would not like to obtain some of these and learn more about this Saviour Jesus Christ, one after another took out his money-bag and purchased, until every Gospel and tract that we had with us had been bought; and then they appointed five of their chief men to escort us politely to our tent, and begged our pardon for the indignities which " this graceless rabble " had put upon us.

This and the one spoken of in the last chapter are two instances of very different treatment met with on our tours. We do not usually meet such eager listening on the one hand, or maltreatment on the other, but we go forward with the work, preaching and scattering that gospel that is showing itself more and more to be " the power of God unto salvation to every one that believeth."

XI. A FRUITFUL PREACHING TOUR.

I AM moved to reproduce here, somewhat abridged, a diary letter written on a long preaching tour in 1872, to give a sample of the varied daily incidents on such a tour and to show how we sometimes reap fruits in our missionary work. The letter was addressed to the secretary of the Board of Foreign Missions of the Reformed Church, and was published in full in the " Intelligencer" of that time.

"RÁYALPÁD, MYSORE, May 23, 1872.

"I am out here at present on another preaching tour. Under the pressure of the terrible reductions forced upon us in January, we feared that we would have to relinquish touring for this year; but enough has come in, in donations from friends in this country, to enable us to resume our preaching tours in an economical way.

"I came to this place, the first stage on the road to Bangalore, just over the boundary in the Mysore kingdom, because there is a little traveler's bungalow here that we can occupy and save the expense of bringing out our tents. Dr. E.C. Scudder and I first visited this region in 1862, just ten years since, and I toured it over again thoroughly in 1867, but have not been able to visit it since until now.

"This morning we were out in a town three and one half miles from here, where I had never before been, and had an unusually nice audience, who all gathered and sat in the village court and veranda, while at their invitation I sat on the magistrate's platform and preached to them of the love of Jesus and His free salvation. As I spoke of what He had done and suffered for us, I noticed a moisture in many eyes, and at the conclusion the village magistrate and the village schoolmaster each purchased a New Testament, while all who could read eagerly bought Gospels and tracts.

"Saturday, May 25th. I rode in yesterday morning twelve miles to Madanapalle, to perform an important operation at the hospital and to attend to other work at the station. After the operation, which I am glad to say turned out well, I preached to the crowd of patients waiting in the hospital veranda, and had, as always there, a most attentive and respectful audience.

"I have reason to be more and more gratified with the aspects of the medical department of my work in this region. The little dispensary, which I began in 1865 in order to bring the villagers to me to hear the truth, when the doctors on account of my jungle fever forbade my going to the villages, has grown on and on until I now have one of the finest up-country hospitals and dispensaries in all the Madras Presidency, second, of course, to our large mission hospital and dispensary at Arcot, but second to few others. As you know, I carried it on entirely on subscriptions raised in India until 1869. It then became so heavy a burden, both in expense and work to be done, that I felt that I could not longer bear it all myself, and at my request the government took it over and established it as a first-class government hospital and dispensary, placing it, however, under my full control; and from that time to this, three years, I have been using it more and more as a missionary hospital.

"I am told now by the authorities at Madras that they regard it still as a mission hospital, for which they are responsible no further than to see that it has all the funds necessary. At my urgent request, however, the deputy inspector-general of the medical department was sent here in February to see and report upon its working. He gave in an exceedingly flattering report, calling special attention to the large percentage of important and successful operations, and the small pecuniary outlay per hundred patients treated. As the result of his visit, we shall receive still greater aid this year from the government.

"During the last month I have had the privilege of receiving two adults into our congregation at Madanapalle, in connection with my dispensary work. One, a man of forty, came from the Kurnool district to the hospital some months ago with what then seemed almost an incurable disease. While in the hospital he received religious instruction with the others, and on his being discharged cured a few weeks since, he gave in his name as a Christian, determined to live and die in the religion by whose agency he believed that his life had been saved. He has obtained employment in Madanapalle, so that he can remain here and receive further instruction and be baptized.

"Tuesday, May 28th. We rose this morning between four and five o'clock, and walked out across the hills five miles to Adakíl. It was my first visit there. Our audience consisted almost entirely of Brahmans and Mohammedans; they listened well and purchased a number of Scriptures and tracts. There is a great change coming over the people, as evidenced by the way they listen to our preaching.

"Day before yesterday, Sunday evening, we preached in the main street of the town of Ráyalpád itself. Twice before when I had been here, in 1862 and 1867, I had found rather turbulent audiences; now one could not ask for a more attentive or polite audience than we found. We began by showing man's lost condition and the insufficiency of their system to redeem a soul from eternal death.

"An aged and respectable Brahman said, 'We will admit all that, sir; now will you not please tell us how we can be saved from hell? That is what we most earnestly desire to know.' And he spoke with real feeling.

"With such a request I tried to set forth, in all its simplicity and loveliness, that wonderful scheme of grace, showing how it was that without a sacrifice for sin there could be no remission, and that Christ had made that one complete sacrifice that was to atone for the sins of the whole world, and how to obtain a share in it. As I finished, the Brahman who had spoken before, and who had followed me most intently all the way through, said to another,' Well, we never heard such wonderful words before; we must examine into it carefully.' And he purchased some of our books and urged others to do the same.

"As soon as we finish this region, which will take ten days more, I expect to take my tents and go out twenty miles northwest of Madanapalle on a medico-evangelistic tour. An English gentle man in this district, who takes great interest in my medical work, has proposed to pay the expenses of such a tour up to Rs 200; and as another has already sent me Rs 100 for the same purpose, I am getting ready my medicines and going out. It is very hard work for one to carry on both medical and evangelistic work in tents, but it pays, and, God willing, I hope to do a good deal of it this year.

"Gattu, June 15th. We completed the tour of which I last wrote on the 5th of June, and returned to Madanapalle to spend the Sabbath there, as it was our communion season. It was an interesting and, I trust, profitable time. We were permitted to receive one adult to the communion on confession of his faith, an educated young man employed under government in the public works department, and five by certificate from other churches. I also baptized one adult and his son, converts from heathenism, who have long been under instruction, and one who had been under suspension was restored. Our Christian congregation at Madanapalle now numbers over one hundred, and, I trust, is growing in all good things.

"After spending the Sabbath at home, and having four days to prepare our chests of medicines, I started out again, June loth, with my native helpers and my traveling dispensary, for a two months' tour in this direction, northwest from Madanapalle. I have with me four native preachers and two medical assistants for dispensing medicines, wishing to be able to preach night and morning in the villages, and to preach to and treat all who come to the tent during the day for medicines.

"Our first camp was at Gattu, a town eighteen miles west by north of Madanapalle. It is a place where we have often toured before, and one near which several villages have at different times promised to come over to Christianity. We are going slowly and thoroughly over the field now, hoping that the time has come when the Lord will give some of them courage and faith to come out on the Lord's side; for we believe they are thoroughly convinced of the truth of Christianity and are only held back by fear from embracing it.

"Gollapalle Tópe, Tuesday, July 16th. We have swung round now to this place, our third encampment on this tour, fifteen miles from Madanapalle on another road, and eight miles from our former encampment. This morning we rose at four o'clock and started before it was fairly light to go to a cluster of villages nestled in among the hills to the north of this, which we had never before reached. After a stony and thorny walk of nearly six miles through the mountain jungle, we came into a valley where a number of villages have been built We preached in all these and were most cordially received. Indeed, I found there some old patients who had been treated by us at Madanapalle, and they seemed almost persuaded to become Christians.

"On reaching my tent again I found a crowd of nearly fifty, who were waiting for treatment, to whom the catechist whom I had left at camp for that purpose had been preaching, and to whom he had given tickets entitling them to treatment, on each of which is printed a concise statement of the way of salvation through Jesus Christ.

"I sat down at once and commenced their treatment. It was after twelve o'clock before I got through with all who were waiting and was able to stop for breakfast. In the afternoon other crowds came. I am having from sixty to one hundred patients daily. To all of these we preach before giving medicines, and find them most willing listeners; and, as almost every patient is accompanied by one or two friends, we preach each day to twice our number of patients at the tent, besides those we reach in the villages.

"Thursday, July 18th. Yesterday we were going out to a market-town six miles through the hills, as it was the weekly market-day there and we wished to preach to the crowds that would assemble; but it commenced raining before 5 a.m. and rained almost continuously through the day. I was surprised, however, to find numbers of patients dropping in through the day in spite of the rain. They had heard that I was soon to move my camp on, and, fearful of missing their chance, they came through the rain for treatment. Today it has been showery, but I have had some seventy patients and was able to go out preaching in the evening.

"I have never, I think, seen such real earnestness in the

reception of our message as now. I cannot help thinking that we are on the eve of an important movement. In this region are numbers of villages where they have been promising us for the last three or four years that they would become Christians. They have renewed the promise from time to time, and I hope some of them are now ready to join us.

"We are going tomorrow morning early to a village of Mála weavers and cultivators three miles from here, which one of the catechists visited a month ago from another encampment, and where some of the people seemed ready to join us. I have, however, gone so many times to villages hoping to receive the people, and found that they had mean-time been frightened into withdrawing again, that I hope with trembling. God grant that this time we may not be disappointed! My six assistants and myself have this even-ing been holding a special prayer-meeting in their behalf, praying that they may have grace and strength given them from on high boldly to confess Christ tomorrow morning.

"Friday evening, July 19th. The morning has dawned, and blessed be God's glorious name for ever and ever; verily our mouths are filled with praise and thanksgiving.

"As we planned yesterday, we went out early this morn-ing to the village of Timmapalle. The people all assembled, small and great, on the smooth granite slope at the base of the rocky hill at the foot of which their village nestled. The catechist to whom they had given their promise a month before first addressed them, urging the fulfilment of their promise; I followed, taking as my theme, '" How long halt ye between two opinions? if the Lord be God, follow Him;" if these your idols be God, then stand by them. The decision should no longer be deferred.' Then Jesus Christ, as the one and all-sufficient Saviour, was lovingly set forth before them.

"When we had finished, the head man of the village, a

gray-haired old patriarch, spoke up: 'Put my name down as a Christian. I at least will no longer halt between two opinions; Jesus Christ must be my Saviour.' After a little his younger brother said, 'Add my name to his.'

"There was a painful pause. I asked,' Is there not another man here that dares to make a third?'

The last man in the audience, a man of thirty, said, 'Yes, sir; I too will be a Christian.' Then others to the number of ten heads of families gave in their names for themselves and families, the women also being there, as the Mala women might be, and agreeing.

"Placing a sheet of paper on the granite boulder by the side of which we had stood in speaking, a covenant was drawn out, in which they covenanted to renounce all their idols, to give up all heathen practices and customs, and to observe the precepts of the gospel so far as they knew them or should be further instructed in them; we, on our part, covenanting to give them a catechist who should reside near them and daily teach them in the way of life, and to establish a school for the education of their children. Then, having commended them in prayer to God Jehovah, whom they had now taken as their God, and promising to come again soon, we left them and came back to our camp.

"They seem well-to-do, earnest men; they have been considering the step long, and we hope they will be firm. There are several more heads of families belonging to the village, who were absent to-day; but they are coming too.

"It was after nine o'clock when we got back to the tent, and I found a crowd of nearly a hundred waiting for medicines. After preaching I commenced treating them, and worked on until twelve o'clock; but finding the crowd growing scarcely perceptibly less, I stopped work for a few minutes and ate my breakfast, while one of the catechists was preaching again to the crowd outside; and then I began once more, having scarcely a moment's rest during the day and not finishing until dark. I have had one hundred and thirty-eight patients to-day, of whom some seventy were new cases, and some of them important ones, which took me much time. It has been a wearying, but intensely interesting, day to me. If the village which joined us this morning stands firm, without a doubt a number of others will join us at once. In fact, several have pledged that as soon as one village came over and stood firm and survived the persecutions they would have, they too would come.

"The arch-fiend will make every effort to make these men turn back, and I have just made arrangements to move our camp tomorrow morning and pitch it close by their village for a couple of weeks, to support and encourage them by our presence.

"I had before promised to go into Madanapalle myself tomorrow to operate on two patients for cataract, whom I have sent in there this week, as such operations cannot be managed in a tent. I shall therefore go in myself early in the morning, but my tent and native helpers will go on to Timmapalle, and I will join them there, God willing, on Monday.

"Timmapalle, Saturday, July 27th. This has been an exceedingly busy and eventful week. I went on horseback to Madanapalle last Saturday morning, as I had proposed, and on getting off my pony at the hospital found everything ready for me, and proceeded to operate at once on a man of standing, a revenue inspector, for cataract, extracting the lens. The operation promises to be a successful one. Other work kept me very busy during the day. On Sunday I preached in our church, and on Monday morning had to attend to matters at the dispensary, and operate on another man for cataract, and was returning home to breakfast, intending then to come out here, when an express messenger reached me from an English gentleman, a government official at Palmanér, thirty-four miles south, begging me to come without a moment's delay and see his wife, who was dangerously ill. He had sent out a bullock coach, posting it for me half-way, in confidence that I would come.

"Much as I desired to come back speedily to this village, I felt it my duty to go. I arrived at Palmanér at 11 p.m. and found the lady indeed very ill, and was obliged to stay in attendance on her until Friday morning before it was safe to leave her. I was very sorry to lose this four days from my tent at this critical time, but as it was a call of duty, and as I received a liberal fee, which will help me bear the expenses of this tour for many days longer, I could not complain. I have had a long horseback ride in the sun today, more than thirty miles, to reach this place, but I felt that I must be back as soon as possible. Since reaching here this evening I have received the names of the remaining eleven families of this village, Timmapalle, and the names of five families from the hamlet of Rázapalle, half a mile north, and the names of nine families of Nalcheruvupalle, one and a half miles northeast. This makes twenty-five families who have given in their names to be Christians today, in addition to the ten before. Pray for us, that the Lord may make these all stanch and steadfast Christians, for they will meet with much persecution.

"Monday, July 29th. The arch-fiend is doing his best, or rather worst, to frighten these people into giving up trying to be Christians. Saturday night and yesterday morning evil-disposed persons from other villages got hold of these people and succeeded in frightening them so, with such pictures of the evils which were sure to come upon them for renouncing their old gods, that some of them actually fled in terror to the jungle and hid all day yesterday; others hid in caves; others barred themselves in their close houses and did no cooking, lest smoke should reveal their presence.

"Only a few had courage to come to my tent for worship in the morning; more came in the evening; and to-day, as they see that no harm has come on them so far, they seem less fearful.

"I expected great difficulty in getting land here for a school-house chapel and native helpers' house, as the land-holders are all banded against us; so the joint magistrate of the district, an English Christian gentleman and one of my warmest supporters, came out here today on purpose to show to the people about here his sympathy in the movement and to secure for us the needed land. I am glad to say we succeeded in getting the very piece I wanted. A necessary surgical operation yesterday, performed on the son of the owner of that piece of ground, helped our negotiations wonderfully.

"Friday, August 2nd. We have begun to erect the building which is to serve both as schoolhouse and church here, for the present, for the villagers near enough to attend here. It is to be of mud or adobe walls, with thatched roof, fifteen by forty feet in size. The people here contribute their labor toward the building and furnish the materials for the roof. The needed money outlay must be met by special donations for the purpose.

"Wednesday, August 7th. Have been on the move again since my last date. Saturday morning early I rode in to the hospital for two more operations and to attend to the location of an additional hospital building, which is to be erected for us by government. Spending Sunday at home, I returned to this place. We are busily engaged in preaching the gospel in all of the towns and villages within five miles of our tent. A steady stream of patients for treatment continues. My evenings I give up to the instruction of new converts, having them in my tent every night. I have also people from the high-caste villages near by, who come into the tent and sit freely side by side with the Mála converts. I have had many interesting conversations with people from the adjacent high-caste villages. My staying here and treating their sick is inclining them to be friendly to the new converts, instead of persecuting them; I hope so, at least.

"Sunday, August 11th. Yesterday was the weekly market-day at the town of Burrakáyalakóta, one mile from here. We were all intending to go there and preach, but I was kept on my cot in the tent by a severe pull of jungle fever. I have been out so much in the sun and wet for the two and a half months of this tour, and with plenty of long, hard rides and walks, that I find myself having an attack of fever every few days. In fact, if I did not hug the quinine bottle pretty closely I would be quite knocked up; and just now I am anxious to be able to look thoroughly after this opening work. I carry a small bottle of quinine in my pocket wherever I go, and am usually able to anticipate and stave off the attack, but yesterday I was floored.

"The native helpers, however, went to the fair and had a very interesting time. At the conclusion of their preaching a respectable, gray-haired old man, a Mála cultivator, came to them and asked after me, saying that he had hoped to meet me there, having heard that we were in this region; for he and his people wanted to become Christians, and he wished to ask me to come to their village and receive them.

"He and his nephew were old patients of mine. His nephew had been brought to my dispensary on a native cot, borne by four men, in 1869, in what seemed a dying condition. A severe surgical operation was the only thing that could save his life. The operation was performed; the young man recovered. For two weeks, while they were there, they and the young man's mother listened attentively to the daily reading of the Word and preaching and prayer in the hospital. On returning to their village they took with them Gospels and tracts, saying that they would never worship their old gods again, and they wanted these books for themselves and their neighbors to read, that they might learn to worship our God. We had meantime lost sight of them, and they now reported that all of their little hamlet were ready to embrace Christianity. Their village is five and a half miles from our present camp.

"This morning at four o'clock my native helpers started for that village. Feeling too weak from yesterday's fever to walk with them, I started somewhat later and went on horseback. As I was passing a village about half-way, riding rapidly to overtake the native helpers, the village magistrate came running out and begged me to stop and see a man suffering intensely from a deep-seated abscess in the sole of his foot. I did so, and opened the abscess with a pocket instrument, gave directions for poulticing, told him to send a man to my tent for medicines, and went on. On arriving at the little hamlet of Nalapórapalle I recognized my two old friends at once, and they seemed very glad to see me. After a very interesting talk with the people, all the six families residing in this little hamlet gave in their names, renouncing heathenism and placing themselves under Christian instruction.

"On our way back we stopped to preach in a number of other villages, where much interest is manifested, and did not reach our tent until near noon, and it was 1 p.m. before we were able to meet for our morning Sabbath service.

Several new faces appeared in the congregation, and the deepest interest was maintained.

"Monday, August 12th. We went this morning to the village a mile and a half north of this, Nalcheruvupalle, the people of which embraced Christianity several days since, had a service with the people, and succeeded in obtaining a good site for erecting a school-house church. While preaching to them the people of the high-caste village adjoining came and sat down and listened most attentively, and at the conclusion promised to send their children for instruction as soon as our Christian school was established.

"The leading men of several of the surrounding villages, including Brahmans, Rájpoots, goldsmiths, merchants, Sudras, have come to my tent to-day to have a talk with me about the 'new religion,' and to express their gratification that we were going to establish a Christian school here. Several, including the magistrate of this village, promise to send their sons.

"Thus far we have received ten villages under Christian instruction. This is the movement of which I wrote you in February, 1869, that I was sure was coming. I have been watching for it, toiling for it, praying for it, and it has come, and I am almost overwhelmed with the greatness of the work that is thrust upon me. How can one missionary alone stand under such a load, precious though that load be? 'The harvest truly is great, but the laborers are few: pray ye therefore the Lord of the harvest, that He would send forth laborers into His harvest;' and not only pray, but oh, ye sworn followers of Christ in America, send forth your sons to gather in His glorious harvest."

Group of Hindu Idols, out of Employment.

XII. OUR VILLAGE CATHEDRAL.

WITHIN a fortnight of the coming over to Christianity of the people of the little village of Timmapalle, we had secured a site, and our first village schoolhouse church was going up before my eyes as I remained there in camp.

The quarter of an acre we had purchased was located one hundred yards north of the northernmost house of the little hamlet, and my tent was pitched in the middle of the lot, between where the church and the house for the catechist were to be. In that I was holding meetings every evening for the instruction of the new converts, and during the day I was treating all patients who came in from surrounding villages, high caste or low caste.

The people of this hamlet, who had now in a body embraced Christianity, were Málas, a low caste among the Telugus, but little higher than the Pariahs among the Tamils; but this did not prevent the highest castes of the region from coming to my tent, pitched adjoining their hamlet, for medical treatment or for religious conversation or discussion.

The new converts had promised to contribute their labor toward the erection of a church, and to supply the material for the roof, several high-caste landholders of the surrounding villages having agreed each to furnish one beam.

As soon as the land was secured the foundation for the church was staked out, forty by fifteen feet. The men, the new converts, came with their native pickaxes, with only one blade each and with a round point and very heavy, so that they could drive them into the stone-like subsoil, and with their shovels, with short handles put to them at right angles like a hoe, and began the excavation.

One span deep they came to the dense clay and gravel subsoil, almost as hard as stone. The women took their earthen water-pots — "pitchers" they are sometimes called in the Bible — on their heads and in single file marched down to the "tank," or dammed pond where water is stored for irrigation, an eighth of a mile distant, and brought up at each trip four or five gallons of water apiece, and poured it into this excavation. The men, throwing in some of the earth they had dug out, tramped it up with their bare feet into a thick clay.

Ten feet away, along the border line of our land, they dug a long trench three feet deep, pouring in water to soften it as they dug. The intensely hard subsoil was mixed with the softer earth they had dug in the foundation, and worked up by feet and hands into rough cubes of half a cubic foot each, and put out upon the ground in the sun to bake, like the adobe of New Mexico. The hot sun baked them hard enough in a day or two to build into the foundation and wall, and the walls began to rise.

In each end was a doorway four feet wide. When the walls were built up with these dried bricks of clay and gravel, or adobe, two and a half feet high, openings two and a half feet wide were left for windows. Rough frames for these windows were made by the village plow-maker, for here they all still use wooden plows like those used by Abraham to plow his fields at Beersheba, and the plow-makers are accustomed to do the rough house-carpentering as well. These frames had male bamboos, that is, bamboos with no holes in them and stronger, framed in them perpendicularly four inches apart for bars.

The windows would have no glass nor Venetian blinds nor shutters of any kind, and these bars were necessary for protection, as otherwise hyenas or jackals or other animals prowling around at night jump in and do damage. I have known of a hyena springing into the unbarred window of a native house, in a warm night when the shutters were open, and seizing the infant from its sleeping mother's breast, spring out again and bound off with the screaming child to the jungle, in spite of anything the aroused household could do.

A yoke of buffaloes with solid, wooden-wheeled cart came driving in one morning with the promised beam from one landholder. It was the trunk of a cocoanut-tree. Another brought a beam of better wood from a dismantled mill for grinding and pressing sugar-cane, much of which is grown in that region, and others followed.

After laying a few feet in height of the adobe walls, the men would leave them for a couple of days to dry, and go to the jungle forests a few miles away, and with their crooked bill-hook axes cut and bring in on their heads saplings for the rafters. Others went to the aloe hedges along the outside of the rice-fields and cut and brought in the leaves, a yard tall, from the outside of the hedges, and with stones pounded out the pulp and secured the long fibres for lashing the wattles on the rafters before putting on the thatch, the larger rafters being tied on with rope made from the fibre of the cocoanut husk; while the women went to the adjacent rocky hills and cut the long, wiry mountain grass and brought it in large, long bundles on their heads for thatch.

When the walls were completed, eight feet high, flat granite slabs were brought, quarried from the hillside by building a fire over the required surface, and pouring on cold water when the rock was heated, and so blistering off the slabs. One of these was placed on top of the adobe wall where each transverse beam was to rest, to give stability and to keep the white ants, which would bore up through the dried bricks, from boring on up into the timbers and destroying the roof.

On the center of these transverse beams seven-foot uprights were erected, and on those the ridgepole was secured. The rafters were tied to this and to wall-plates, placed, however, on the transverse beams a foot outside of the walls, to make wide eaves, that would protect the clay walls from the drenching rains during the monsoon. The wattles were tied on these with the aloe fibre. The women brought up more water and thoroughly moistened the long mountain grass so that it would pack more compactly in thatching, one or two practised hands tied on the thatch as it was tossed up to them in small bundles, and the roof was complete.

We had wanted to call in men of the hereditary caste of well- and tank-diggers and wall-builders, as there was so much work in the building of the walls; but they would not come unless we would let them sacrifice to their gods on the spot a sheep or a kid, or at least a fowl, so that their gods would protect them from accident during the building, which, of course, we would not allow.

The walls and roof were at last ready. The plow-maker shaped the rough mango planks we had bought into double doors for the front and rear. The women made a rough mortar, Hindu fashion, from clay and sand and cow dung mixed, and, with the palms of their hands for trowels, plastered the adobe walls within and without, and then whitewashed them, using brushes made from the stems of date-tree leaves. The men brought in more of the moist clay gravel from the trench, and laying it a span deep over the ground inside the walls, pounded it down with rammers made from the palmyra-tree, and made a smooth kind of concrete floor; and then the women brought, in little baskets on their heads, clean-washed sand from the bed of the adjacent stream, and spread it half an inch thick over the floor for a carpet.

A camp-table for pulpit and a chair for the preacher were placed in it, and our new cathedral was complete.

This was the first of the villages that had come over, and quite central; so we erected here the largest and most costly of all our village buildings, — larger than needed for this little hamlet, — that we might here hold our special services and our quarterly meetings, and here administer the Lord's Supper for all this circle. So this is "our cathedral."

On the Sunday morning the head of each family comes, bringing rolled up a date mat or a coarse black goat's-hair blanket rug, and spreads it down on the sand for himself and sons to sit on; this is their "pew "; while the wife brings another and places it on the other side of the church for herself and daughters and the women of her house to occupy; for in these little village churches, according to the custom of the country, the men must sit on one side and the women apart on the other.

In this building during the week our day-school is held. The old-time custom of the country requires village schools to begin at sunrise and, with an hour intermission at noon, close when it is too dark longer to see the books.

We compromised the matter by having school from 7 a.m. to 12 noon, and from 1 to 5 p.m.

The alphabet class requires no text-books; they sit on the sanded floor, and watching the teacher make a letter in the sand with his finger, they make it after him, thus learning reading and writing at the same time.

Every evening this new church is used for "village prayers"; for the unlearned villagers, unable most of them to conduct "family prayers" in their own houses, come together here for evening worship.

The catechist, or the schoolmaster in villages where there is no catechist, makes a good deal of the evening prayers. Besides reading and expounding a chapter in the Bible and offering prayer, concluding with the Lord's Prayer, in which all the people join, he drills old and young in the catechism, and teaches them to sing the beautiful Telugu Christian lyrics, and right heartily do they sing.

Some months after the erection of this our cathedral, we held in it a special service, that comes lovingly to my memory. A meeting of our Telugu Bible Revision Committee, of which I was chairman, was being held at Madanapalle, at which delegates were present for several weeks from the different missionary societies laboring in the Telugu country. One Saturday evening several of us went out twenty miles to Timmapalle for the Sabbath service. The people of the adjacent villages had been invited to gather there.

In the early morning they began to arrive, and more and more came. We missionaries were seated in camp-chairs against the rear wall, and the camp-table pulpit drawn up close to us to save room. Our native assistants were seated on a rug at our right. The people came in and were seated in rows across the building cross-legged, native fashion, and so close together that their shoulders touched. The knees of the second row touched the backs of those in the front row, and thus the church was packed. The people were so compact that a rat could not have made its way from front to rear, and those who could not get in were listening from the outside through the open doors and windows.

My English brother missionary of the Church of England took the morning service. He was a fine singer of Telugu lyrics, and when that whole congregation, of those who were one year ago worshipers of Vishnu and of idols, joined in hymning the praises of Jesus with reverent air and hearty voice, he seemed to be carried away by it into another land, and his earnest sermon of such spiritually uplifting power was an index of where his thoughts had been.

The afternoon sermon was by my American Baptist colleague, and was a fit sequel to the sermon of the morning. The evening service was conducted by one of still another denomination, and was followed by earnest personal talks with the many who lingered for a further word.

At midnight, as we were getting into our coach to return for our morning work at Madanapalle, my English Episcopal friend said to me, " I have heard more artistic singing of the praises of Immanuel in some of the famed churches of my dear old England, but none that I believe went straighter to the throne of God or sounded more sweet to our Redeemer. I have greatly enjoyed many services in England's grand cathedrals, but never so much as these of to-day among the newly redeemed ones in this your village cathedral."

XIII. The Building and Opening of a Free Reading Room.

FOR a long time we had tried in vain to obtain the slightest foothold within the thickly built native town of Madanapalle. The Telugus are always courteous and kind to strangers, and so long as we remained outside of the town they were friendly and helpful. The very few European houses so far built here are located on the opposite side from the town of a little river or creek, which is dry except during the early and the late rainy seasons. Our house is built here, and our temporary mud-wall and thatched-roof place of worship was of necessity placed here also, as we could not get a place nearer the people.

I had long ago determined to secure, if possible, by purchase or for rent, one of the town bazaars or small stores, or to buy one of the very few vacant lots and build and open a free reading-room, which should, be well stocked with vernacular and English newspapers, gazettes, magazines, and books, and to use that for evening preaching one day in the week, so as to get hold of the educated portion of the non-Christian community, to whom we had not thus far gained as close access as we had desired.

My every effort had been foiled. When in passing through the streets I found that a bazaar or store had been vacated, and learned that its owners were in the habit of renting it, I would quietly enter into negotiations to rent it. Nothing is done by Hindus without due, or rather undue, deliberation, and although I would accede to the owner's terms, there must be further delay before the papers were drawn out. The other Hindus would learn of it and bring such pressure to bear on the owner that he would back out of his not yet signed contract.

I offered double rent, but no owner dared to let me have a place. A bazaar was for sale; I learned the price and tendered the money; it was refused. The owner came secretly to see me, saying that he would be glad to sell it to me, but that all his caste people would boycott him if he did. I offered him double the price; no, he would be turned out of his caste if he let me have it.

At last, in 1870, my opportunity came. A corner lot on one of the main streets, opposite the post-office, had been for years in litigation. The old building on it had tumbled down. It was one of the best sites in the whole town for a reading room and evangelistic hall. The case in the chief district court eighty miles away was decided, and a decree was issued ordering the lot, a small one, to be sold by public auction, and the proceeds divided in a certain way between the contending heirs.

Even now I could not appear openly as a purchaser, nor could any of our native Christians nor any one known to be in my employ bid openly on it, or a combination would be formed and it would be run up to twenty times its value to prevent our getting a footing in the streets of the town.

There was a young Brahman assistant in the English magistrate's office now living in town, who had attracted my attention as a man of intelligence, of excellent character, and of independence. I invited him to come to my house and see me, and explained to him my plans for opening a free reading-room; told what Telugu, Tamil, Kanarese, Maráthi, Hindustani, and English periodicals, and what government gazettes, and what maps, dictionaries, encyclopedias, and books of history, travel, and science I proposed to put in for the free use of all who chose to make that their literary center, with ample conveniences for writing and for study. He became very much interested in the project and said it would be an unspeakable boon to the town.

I told him I would do all this if he had the courage to go to the auction and bid in that corner lot in his own name, pay for it on the spot with money I would put in his hands for the purpose, have the papers made out there by the court officers in his own name to avoid interference, and then transfer the title to me and have the transaction completed beyond recall before any one suspected what he bought the lot for, so that they would see that interference would be in vain and would not trouble him so much. I told him that probably all his co-religionists would curse him at first, but that within two months after the reading-room was opened, and they experienced its advantages, they would bless him still more heartily and lastingly, and that it all depended now on whether he had backbone enough to undertake the matter, and pledged that I would do all in my power to shield him from serious abuse.

He sat for a few moments in deep thought, and then, straightening himself up, he said, with determination manifest in every feature, "Yes, sir, I will do it; you shall have the deeds of that lot in your hands before midnight."

I placed in his hands double the highest sum we thought the lot would bring, so that he need not have to send to me for more and so reveal the source of his supply. The sale was to take place at noon. The day was one of prayer on the part of my three native assistants, to whom alone I had revealed my scheme, and myself, that there might be no slip, but that the gospel might thus gain a home within the busy town.

As soon as it was dark that evening my Brahman friend appeared with face radiant, if a little anxious, saying, "I have succeeded. Here is the deed for the land in your name, and here is the certificate from the registrar that the deed has been registered; for he is a friend of mine, and stopped after office hours to register it himself after his clerks had gone. He is pledged to secrecy, and no one outside suspects what the lot has been purchased for, and here is the balance of the money you placed in my hands. You will erect and open the reading-room quickly, will you not? so that the period of abuse from my co-religionists may be as brief as possible."

I thanked him heartily, told him I would endeavor to see that he never regretted the bold stand he had taken, and that he would himself be surprised to see the prompt developments.

I had building going on at the hospital with a building *maistry*, or overseer, and a corps of masons, carpenters, and coolies, whom I could transfer at once to another work if I saw fit. Word had come to me at three o'clock that the lot had been knocked down to my friend as the highest bidder, and I had lost no time in making my arrangements. I had sent for a stone contractor whom I employed, and he had engaged to have thirty cart-loads of foundation stone standing in carts at my gate at daylight the next morning, to be dumped wherever my maistry should tell him, and to deliver thirty more during the day. The brick contractor had made a similar contract, and the lime contractor another. My maistry had agreed with his whole staff of workmen to be on hand at the first dawn of day and work right through for a double day's pay; and before I retired that night my plans were all completed and arrangements all made for a rapid stroke.

At day-dawn the whole force met at the hospital and marched down quietly into the town, with a few cart-loads of mortar already mixed; the excavation at one corner of the front wall was rapidly made by twenty coolies; the thirty cartloads of stone were driven there and unloaded, and as the sun peeped over the horizon the masons were laying the stones for the corner. The bricks and mortar came, and before the people of the town were astir six feet in length of the foundation had been completed and several courses of bricks had been laid on that, while the bottom courses of stone had been laid across the whole front and the excavations for the side walls were rapidly going on.

The people rubbed their eyes and gazed in astonishment. What this meant no one could divine. They knew that the Brahman had bought the lot the preceding afternoon and at first supposed that he was rapidly building a house. The maistry refused to say anything; the busy swarm of workmen did not know.

By ten o'clock the front walls were two feet high, and then I appeared upon the scene, for I had not been seen there after the sun had risen, and told the gathering spectators what I proposed to put there, and that when the reading-room was opened they themselves would be very glad that they had been outwitted; that there was no possible way of stopping me now, for I would carry it through at any cost; that I held a registered deed of the lot in my hand, and the English chief magistrate had promised to see that I was not molested. After a little consultation among themselves they agreed to refrain from hopeless interference and wait and see what this new reading-room would be.

Our English friends, officials in the judicial, revenue,

engineering, and police departments who had themselves or their families received medical treatment from me, came forward and liberally contributed the funds for this new undertaking, and in an incredibly short time for India the building of one story, with flat masonry roof that could not be burned, was completed and ready to enter.

It stands on a street corner. The lot is only twenty feet wide by forty long. In the front is one wide door, and at the side wide windows only four or five feet apart, and a veranda of five feet width on both streets, so that when doors and windows are all thrown wide open those in the verandas can hear a speaker as well as those inside, and most of them can see him.

The room is matted with grass mats, and in the center is a writing-table with inkstands and writing materials always ready. Arranged along the sides are narrow tables with newspapers in the different languages, magazines, and government gazettes on them, together with a copy of the Bible in each of the seven languages more or less read here.

At the farther end are two glass-door bookcases; the one filled with dictionaries in the different languages, encyclopedias, and books for reading, including works on history, travels, poetry, morals, and science, the most of them being in English, but including all I could lay my hands on of an improving nature in Telugu, Tamil, Kanarese, with a few in Hindustani, Maráthi, and Sanskrit. These are free to any one to take and read when he pleases.

The other bookcase is filled with Scriptures, tracts, school-books, and Christian literature in the various languages, for sale. A supply of stationery also, and all requisites for school use, are kept; and by supplying Christian school-books here at cost, or less, we are introducing them into many a non-Christian school of this region in place of their more expensive school-books and cumbersome *olas*, or palm-leaf manuscript school-books now in use.

This reading-room is opened daily, excepting Sundays, at 2 p.m., and kept open until 9 p.m.; and as the bright light shines out on to two streets it attracts many to come and sit and read who would otherwise sit on their verandas in idle talk or gossip.

On Wednesday evening of each week we have a Bible lecture here. It is in Telugu and is designed to lead the thinking non-Christians to a more intelligent appreciation of the beauties and stores of wisdom contained in God's revealed Word, and to more of a love for and reverence of that Book of books. I try to make the lecture as interesting as I can, and never allow myself to exceed half an hour, so as not to weary them.

Ten minutes before the time appointed for the lecture our native assistants go there and commence singing some of their beautiful Christian songs in Telugu melodies. This is the signal for assembling, so that when I get there I always find both the building and the veranda already filled. I then read the passages I have selected from the Telugu Bible and lecture from it, always closing with a short prayer for the divine blessing on the words spoken.

I have thus far never once been interrupted by talking or unseemly conduct, and the most profound silence is observed during the prayer. The audience has averaged over one hundred and fifty each Wednesday evening thus far, and we cannot help feeling that good is being done.

As soon as the building was completed and furnished, even before the walls were fully dry, we sent around a notice to the principal native gentlemen of the place, telling them that on a certain evening the new reading-room would be opened and its purposes and rules explained, and inviting all to be present.

A number of English gentlemen, who had given us liberal pecuniary aid in the erection of the building, now gave us their countenance and assistance in the opening of it, the joint magistrate of the district making an address in English, which was interpreted for those who understood only Telugu by the Brahman interpreter of his court. The chief officer of the revenue settlement of the district, an English gentleman, made an address in Telugu; this was followed by a neat address from my Brahman friend, telling of the profit which he believed this reading-room would be to himself and them all, and telling them why he had assisted me in the purchase of the lot.

An address in Telugu was also made by myself, in which I told the people that, while this was designed as a means of intellectual improvement, I did not wish to disguise the hope I entertained that it would prove also a means of spiritual improvement to many of them by bringing them to the feet of Him who is the Author and Giver of spiritual life, even Him who is revealed in the Christian Scriptures; and urged them to search the Scriptures which they would find, each in his own language, upon the tables, and see whether there was nothing in them worthy of their sincere acceptance. The building and verandas were packed with attentive listeners, and many stood in the street within hearing, unable to get into even the veranda.

Our record shows that the number who avail themselves of the privileges of the reading-room has thus far averaged not less than ninety a day. Some come just to look at the Madras daily newspapers or the government gazettes, others to read historical works, others to consult the dictionaries, atlases, and books of reference, while many, after finishing the work for which they came, will quietly take up and read a copy of the Bible, and often purchase Scriptures or portions of Scripture in their own languages or in English, to take away and examine at their own houses. Scarcely a day passes without more or less tracts or Scriptures being sold.

A very singular address by a Brahman gentleman has just been made in the reading-room, of which I must give a report in the next chapter.

XIV. A Brahman on the Bible.

A N incident occurred this (Wednesday) evening in our new reading-room, which has made a profound impression on my mind.

On each Wednesday evening we have here a lecture on the Bible, designed for educated non-Christian audiences. A parable, a miracle, a biography, a sermon of Christ, a historical account, as of the creation, the deluge, Joseph in Egypt, the exodus, a prophecy of the Old Testament and its fulfillment in the New, is taken up and illustrated. While it is endeavored to make the lecture attractive as a literary treat, the bearing of the subject on the gospel of Jesus Christ and His salvation is never lost sight of. This evening my subject was, "The law of the Lord is perfect," showing the sufficiency of the Christian Scriptures, but the insufficiency of the Hindu Vedas, to make the soul of sinful man at peace with holy God.

At the close of the lecture, which was attentively listened to by an audience of one hundred and eighty, composed of Brahmans, merchants, farmers, artisans, officials, and students, and which I concluded with a short prayer, as I took my hat to come away, a Brahman, one of the best educated in the place, arose and politely asked permission to say a few words. I, of course, as politely assented and took my seat again, thinking that he probably was designing to attack the position that I had taken, and I said to myself, "

I shall have a sharp discussion with this man, for he is one of the most learned men in the place and a ready speaker; but I have reserve ammunition in abundance on this topic, which I must bring forward and stand to my guns."

To my surprise, however, in a neat address of ten or fifteen minutes, couched in choice and ornate language and with apt illustrations, he urged upon his fellow-citizens the importance of availing themselves of the advantages offered for their intellectual and moral advancement by this reading-room, and in conclusion gave the following *remarkable testimony to the Christian Scriptures*. He spoke in Telugu, but it made such an impression on my mind that I have come home and written it off in as accurate a translation as possible into English. It was as follows:

"Behold that mango-tree on yonder roadside! Its fruit is approaching to ripeness. Bears it that fruit for itself or for its own profit? From the moment the first ripe fruits turn their yellow sides toward the morning sun until the last mango is pelted off, it is assailed with showers of sticks and stones from boys and men and every passer-by, until it stands bereft of leaves, with branches knocked off, bleeding from many a broken twig' and piles of stone underneath, and clubs and sticks lodged in its boughs, are the only trophies of its joyous crop of fruit. Is it discouraged? Does it cease to bear fruit? Does it say, 'If I am barren no one will pelt me and I shall live in peace '? Not at all. The next season the budding leaves, the beauteous flowers, the tender fruit, again appear. Again it is pelted and broken and wounded, but goes on bearing, and children's children pelt its branches and enjoy its fruit.

"That is a type of these missionaries. I have watched them well and have seen what they are. What do they come to this country for? What tempts them to leave their parents, friends, and country and come to this, to them an unhealthy, climate? Is it for gain or for profit that they come? Some of us country clerks in government offices receive more salary than they. Is it for the sake of an easy life? See how they work, and then tell me. No; they seek, like the mango tree, to bear fruit for the benefit of others, and this, too, though treated with contumely and abuse from those they are benefiting.

"Now look at this missionary! He came here a few years ago, leaving all and seeking only our good. He has met with cold looks and suspicious glances, and was shunned, avoided, and maligned. He sought to talk with us of what he told us was the matter of most importance in heaven or earth, and we would not listen; but he was not discouraged. He started a dispensary, and we said, 'Let the Pariahs take his medicines; we won't;' but in the times of our sickness and distress and fear we had to go to him, and he heard us. We complained if he walked through our Brahman streets; but ere long, when our wives and daughters were in sickness and anguish, we went and begged him to come even into our inner apartments, and he came, and our wives and our daughters now smile upon us in health. Has he made any money by it? Even the cost of the medicines has not been returned to him.

"And now, in spite of our opposition, he has bought this site, and built this beautiful room, and furnished it with the choicest of lore in many languages, and put in it newspapers and periodicals, which were inaccessible to us before, but which help us now to keep up with the world around us and understand passing events; and he has placed here tables to write on, and chairs to sit on, and lamps for us to read and write by in the evening; and what does he get for all this? Does he make money by this free reading-room? Why, we don't even pay for the lamp-oil consumed by night as we read.

"Now, what is it makes him do all this for us? *It is his Bible.* I have looked into it a good deal at one time and another, in the different languages I chance to know. It is just the same in all languages — *the Bible.* There is nothing to compare with it in all our sacred books for goodness and purity and holiness and love and for motives of action.

"Where did the English-speaking people get all their intelligence and energy and cleverness and power? It is their Bible that gives it to them. And now they bring it to us and say, 'This is what raised us; take it and raise yourselves.' They do not force it upon us, as the Mohammedans did with their Koran, but they bring it in love, and translate it into our languages, and lay it before us and say,' Look at it, read it, examine it, and see if it is not good.' Of one thing I am convinced: do what we will, oppose it as we may, it is the Christians' Bible that will, sooner or later, work the regeneration of this land."

I could not but be surprised at this testimony thus borne. How far the speaker was sincere I cannot tell; he had every appearance of a man speaking his earnest convictions. Some three years ago I had attended in his zenana his second wife, a beautiful girl, through a dangerous illness, and I knew that he felt very grateful; but I was not prepared to see him come out before such an audience with such testimony to the power and excellency of the Bible. My earnest prayer is that not only his intellect may be convinced, but that his heart may be reached by the Holy Spirit, and that he and many like him may soon become earnest followers of Jesus the Christ.

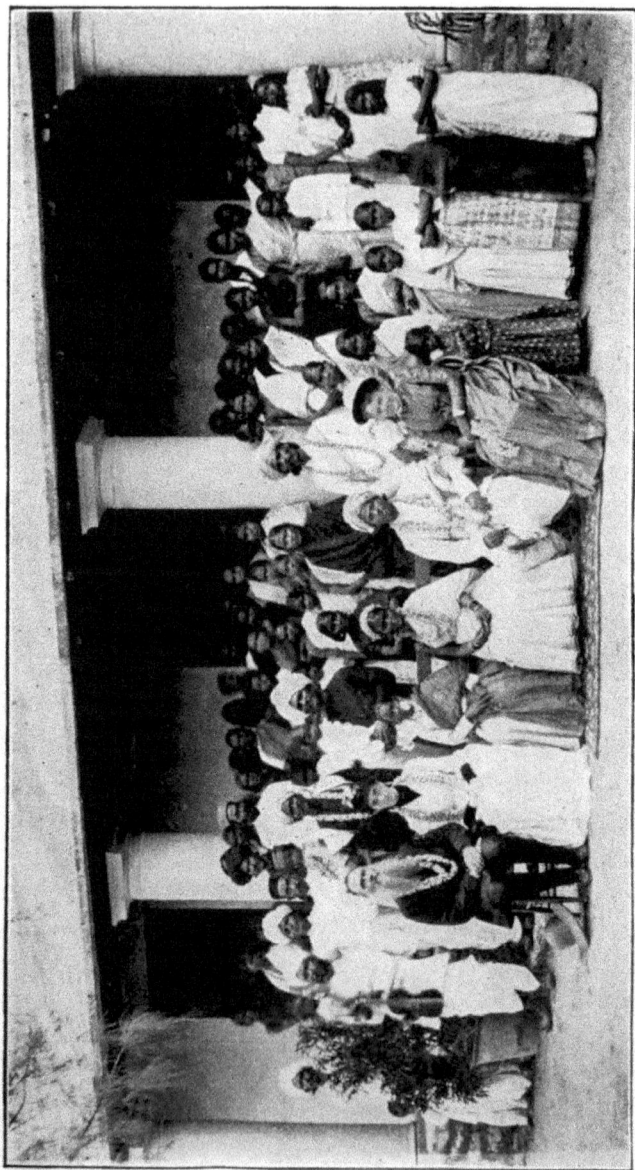

NATIVE CHRISTIAN WEDDING GROUP, MADANAPALLE, 1891,
Girls' Boarding School in Rear.

XV. The Village Magistrate's Death.

A T the Wednesday evening biblical lectures for non-Christians at our free reading-room there was one countenance that we always expected to see.

The *gráma reddi*, or village magistrate, Musalappa by name, always came early and took his seat by the second window on the right from the speaker's desk. He listened with apparent pleasure to the preliminary gospel song service, and when the speaker rose to read from the Christians' Bible and to give a lecture on the passage read, be it a parable, a miracle, a history, a prophecy, a sermon of our Lord, the fixedness of his attention always attracted the notice of the speaker, and his reverent mien during the concluding prayer made one feel that he was silently joining in its petitions.

He was a cousin of the man whose hand and arm had been so fearfully crushed under the wheel of the idol-car shortly after we located at Madanapalle, as they were drawing it in its annual outing late at night. He was one of those who ran to my house and waked me and begged me to come and see if I could save the man's life, for he was dying with nervous shock and loss of blood. The man's life was saved; the ten fractures in his fingers, hand, and forearm were set and united, so that he again had the use of his right hand; and neither he nor his brothers or cousins ever joined again in those heathen festivities, and some of them were often seen at our Sabbath services in church.

Musalappa was one of them. When the reading-room was opened and the weekly biblical lectures for non-Christians were begun, he seemed to be glad to have a chance to listen to Christian teaching without mingling in a Christian congregation and drawing on himself the adverse criticism of his co-religionists.

He was a very quiet, sedate, reticent man, whose character was respected by all. His attentive, earnest countenance, both in our church on his occasional attendance there and weekly at the reading-room, made me feel that the truth was gaining an entrance to his mind and heart. He seemed to avoid giving me any chance to speak to him personally, and I was content to let him continue to drink in the truth weekly at our services, fearing that he would be driven away if I personally pressed the truth home.

A year had passed from the opening of the reading-room. In August of last year, 1871, there was an epidemic of cholera, and of smallpox at the same time, and a number of cases of typhoid fever in the town. My assistant in the hospital was absent on a vacation and I was driven with work beyond measure.

One morning, as I was sitting at the dispensing-table in the hospital, Musalappa came in and sank upon a seat exhausted. I saw that he was very ill and went to him at once. He said he had been very sick for a week or more; that he had asked his brothers — for they and their families all lived together in one house as one family — to ask me to come and treat him, or to bring him to the hospital in a coach or palanquin, but they had absolutely refused and called in native doctors; that he was sure he was fast getting much worse; and that that morning, when they were all out of the house, he had got up and, unnoticed, stolen away on foot to the hospital for me to prescribe for him. I did all that could be done, giving him medicines for the day and night, and sent him home in a conveyance, promising to come the next morning to his house and see him.

I was quite at a loss to account for his family so objecting to his coming to me for treatment, as many of them have been to me for treatment at different times.

The next morning and daily I went to see him, though I was so driven with work that I could go but once each day and then make but a very brief visit. A crowd gathered around the moment I went into his room every time I called, and, as I now see, seemed to wish to prevent my talking with him any more than to prescribe. I could not but notice that there was an unusual commotion about the house, which I could not explain. It was typhoid fever, and he died in spite of all that could at that late stage be done for him.

One of his cousins now tells me that during his sickness he was talking continually of Jesus Christ and of Christianity, saying that it was true and they must embrace it; and I now think that it was their fear that he would openly embrace Christianity before his death, and bring a stigma on them, that made them keep him so long from coming to me, and so guarded when I was present.

I spoke to him generally on the subject of death and of Him whom alone we could trust in such an hour, but did not press it home so personally as I would had I then suspected what I now believe to be the fact.

When I spoke to him of Christ they prevented his replying, as I now recall to mind. His cousin now tells me that during the night before he died, after incoherent talking of Jesus and His salvation for some time, he suddenly rose to a sitting posture in bed and called out with a clear voice, *"The glory of Jesus Christ is filling the whole world, and we must all bow before it. He is the divine Redeemer."*

And so he died. I cannot tell certainly whether he was one of the spiritual fruits of the reading-room, whether to count him among Christ's trophies, or not; but I rejoice unspeakably that "the Lord knoweth them that are His." He will not overlook any of His jewels.

I shall look for him when, through the blood of that Jesus, I am permitted to join the throng of the redeemed, for I trust he will be there.

XVI. Narasappa's Mother, or Christ's Hidden Ones.

YES, I think we do sometimes get glimpses of some of Christ's hidden ones, and believe that Narasappa's mother was one of them.

It was in July, 1872, that my tent was pitched in yonder mango grove, a mile from this place, Gollapalle, where I am now encamped. I had my dispensary tent and was endeavoring to imitate my Master, "going about all the cities and villages, preaching the gospel of the kingdom, and healing every sickness and every disease among the people" as far as possible, with the use of remedies and by the blessing of God upon them.

At sunrise every morning I went out to preach in some adjacent village, returning by eight o'clock to find my tent surrounded by patients waiting for treatment. We first preached to them that "gospel of the kingdom" and then treated their diseases.

One morning my attention was attracted to a nice old Brahman lady, who had brought a little child, her grandson, for treatment. I noticed her listening very earnestly to the preaching. My heart was drawn out toward her. I treated the child, and told her to bring him again the next day. She did, and for several mornings after. She was always on hand to hear the preaching. I learned that she was from this village and that she was the mother of Narasappa, one of the Brahman village officials. The child recovered, and I lost sight of her for the time.

That was the year when the solid ranks of heathenism here began to break and the people of a number of villages of the working classes came out and embraced Christianity. Among others the Mála weavers of a hamlet adjacent to this village asked to be taken under instruction, giving up all their idols. We received them.

We wanted land to build a thatched schoolhouse church upon. One of the Brahman village officials helped us to get it. I knew not why, but afterward learned that he was the son of my old lady friend. A catechist with a very estimable wife was placed there. Their house was midway between the caste village and the Málas' houses. This old lady was one of the first to befriend them. Through her influence they were allowed to draw water at the village caste well, and received many other kindnesses through her friendship. She always came and listened earnestly to the preaching when I came to the village.

I was taken sick and had to go to America. For three years this region was without a missionary. The native assistants were one after another drafted off to meet pressing calls in the Tamil field of our mission. This place was left without a mission helper. The famine came with its fearful desolation. The poor Mála weavers were scattered in search of work and food. After my return to India, in 1878, I came here to rake over the ashes and see if there was any fire left. I found enough to make me rejoice, and reoccupied the station.

I saw the Brahman official who had been kind to us, and who seemed delighted at our return. I asked for his mother; she had died during the famine, but he brought the little boy whom I had treated to see me. I could not ask of him the questions I wished to ask about his mother, but after some

months I saw the catechist who had occupied the station and
to whose wife the old Brahmanee had been such a friend.
His eyes were moist as he told me what had transpired with
reference to the old lady after I went to America.

She had continued her friendliness to them openly, and
used secretly to come to their house by night to talk of Christ
and His salvation. Often, he tells me, late in the evening,
as they were about to retire and the streets were deserted
for the night, they would hear a gentle knock at their door;
on going to open it, they would find their Brahman friend.

She would slip quietly in, close the door, and say, "Now
tell me some more of Jesus;" and as they finished for the
night, "Oh, I do believe in Him, but my Brahman son would
kill me if I should break caste and join you Christians openly;
or if he did not, it would ruin him, for the other Brahmans
would cast him out. I *can't* come out openly and embrace
Christ as my Saviour, but you must let me come very often
and hear you talk about Him, for I do believe in Him."

When that catechist and his wife removed from the place
the secret parting was a very affecting one. "For who will
tell me more of the Lord of life?" was the plaint of the dear
old Brahman lady. Before my return and before the village
had again been occupied by a mission helper she had been
called away; but our Jesus, He who bore our griefs, He
who was tempted like as we are, knew all about her, all her
struggles, and how terrible are the bonds of caste, which she
could not in her widowed old age summon courage to break.
I think of her whenever I come to this village as perhaps
one of the fruits of our work here, and I look forward to
the time when, among those arrayed in white robes, I may
find her and learn that she was indeed, while in this hard
and sinful world, *one of Christ's hidden ones.*

XVII. An Audience of Monkeys.

THE most singular audience that I ever saw gathered to listen to preaching was an audience of monkeys.

When I first commenced work in the region which I have now occupied for more than thirty years, I asked two fellow-missionaries to join me in a preaching tour in the adjacent táluk, or county. We first went with three native assistants to the táluk town, or county-seat. Our tents were pitched in a grove adjoining the town. We usually on our tours went two and two to preach in the villages, but, this being the táluk town and the first time of our preaching the gospel in that region, we went in a body into the native city.

Walking through the cloth, spice, grain, and iron merchants' bazaar streets, and then through the goldsmiths' and silversmiths' street, around through the temple street, and then through the street of Brahman residences, to advertise our presence and incite curiosity to know what we were about, we finally took our stand in the Brahman street and all joined in singing one of the beautiful Telugu Christian lyrics, and gathered an audience of interested listeners.

We stood upon a little raised platform on one side of the street against the house walls. The houses were all of one story, joined together like a city block, with flat roofs and a low parapet along the front of the roof. One of our native assistants read a portion from the Gospels and another preached briefly; then one of my fellow missionaries followed, preaching more at length, while I watched the audience to study the countenances of the people among whom I expected to work.

I had noticed that behind the houses on the opposite side of the street there was a long row of trees growing in their back yards, the branches of which stretched out over the flat roofs.

Chancing to raise my eyes, I noticed many branches of these trees beginning to bend downward toward the roofs, and saw the faces of some old jack-monkeys peering out through the foliage. Soon some of them jumped down and came forward to see what their "big brothers" in the street were about as they stood gazing so intently at these white men standing on the platform. Springing upon the parapet, they seated themselves with their hind feet hanging over in front, and gazing with fixedness at the preacher as they saw the people in the street doing.

Other monkeys followed until there was a long row of them thus seated on the parapet. The late-comers I could see walking along behind the parapet, looking for a place wide enough to get a seat. Failing to find a place between two already seated monkeys wide enough, they would put up their hands and, pushing each one sidewise, would seem to be saying, "Sit along a little, please, and give a fellow a seat," until the "bench" was crowded.

The audience in the street, standing with their backs toward that row of houses, did not notice the monkeys, and so their attention was not distracted by them; the preacher went on with his sermon; the monkeys sat demurely, listening as intently as the audience in the street.

I had noticed that many mother monkeys had brought their babies to church with them. These little baby monkeys sat upon the thigh of the mother, while her hand was placed around them in a very human fashion; but the sermon was evidently too high for these little folks to comprehend. Glancing up, I saw one of the little monkeys cautiously reach his hand around and, catching hold of another baby monkey's tail, give it a pull. The other little monkey struck back, but each mother monkey evidently disapproved of this levity in church, and each gave its own baby a box on the ears as though saying, "Sit still! Don't you know how to behave in church?" The little monkeys, thus reprimanded, turned the most solemn faces toward the preacher and seemed to listen intently to what he was saying.

With the exception of a monkey now and then trying to catch a flea that was biting him in some tender spot, they thus sat demurely until the preacher finished his sermon, and until we had distributed Gospels and tracts among the audience, and, bidding them a polite farewell, had started for our tents.

Our "celestial audience," seeing our " terrestrial audience" dispersing, then, and not until then, left their seats and demurely walked back and sprang upon the branches again. There were no "monkey capers" as they went; they were as serious as a congregation leaving a church, and sat upon the branches in a meditative mood as though thinking over what they had heard the preacher say. And thus we left our unique monkey audience.

THE MISSION CHURCH, MADANAPALLE.

XVIII. The Stick-to-it Missionary.

I HAVE seen him, and the interview did me good. I met him thirty miles from the border of Thibet, when on my tramp in Bhutan and independent Sikkim in May, 1892. He is a Roman Catholic missionary, but my hour's interview with him confirmed the impression I had received from others that he was a godly, evangelical, zealous Christian missionary.

I have seen other such evangelical missionaries connected with the Romish Church. I met one in Jerusalem in 1874, with whom I had very many hours of intimate communion, as day by day he came to me and asked me to tell him more of my missionary life in India, of our opportunities, our labors, our trials, our hindrances, our successes. How earnestly did he rejoice over our successes, in his joy at hearing of heathen brought to accept of Jesus Christ as their Saviour seeming to be perfectly oblivious of the fact that his church branded me as a heretic! And when, after a week of such pleasant Christian intercourse, I left him to go on my journey, he threw both arms around my neck, and kissed me on one cheek and on the other, and with tears in his eyes he bade me good-by until we should meet before the great white throne, each with his sheaves garnered for the Master.

I met such a one years ago in India, I am thankful to say, of the purity and holiness of whose life hundreds were ready to bear loving testimony, and who on his death-bed requested that he might see me, telling his attendant priest that he and that American missionary had in years gone by had such pleasant spiritual intercourse, and now he wished to see me once more before we should meet in those " many mansions."

Yes, I thank God that the Church of Rome, with all its superincumbent superstitions and errors, cannot prevent some born in her communion and working under her orders from coming out into the clearer light and working for God and for souls, relying solely on Jesus Christ as the way and the truth and the life. And such a one I think I found on the borders of Thibet, who had for thirty-six consecutive years been trying to effect an entrance into that kingdom to carry into its darkness the light of the gospel.

He gave me his history. It helped me; it will help others. In 1856, thirty-six years before, Father Andrew D —, having completed a thorough training in the schools of the Propaganda, was sent out to India commissioned as "missionary apostolic to Thibet," and was directed to gain an entrance into that sealed kingdom from India. He came to Darjeeling and tried to secure an entrance, but was driven back. He went to northwest India, to the hill states lying between Simla and Afghanistan, and early in 1857 succeeded in crossing the border, but was arrested and sent back to Agra. The mutiny came on. He was foiled in every attempt to cross the border, and came near losing his life several times.

In 1858 he received orders to sail to Canton and try to effect an entrance through China. He went up the river from Canton and, pressing on, made an entrance, but was soon arrested and with indignities sent back to Canton. He spent another year studying the Thibetan language and customs, being joined by two other priests, who were to go with him as his assistants. After a year's study, investigation, and preparation, they started up the river again as Chinese traders, having adopted Chinese costume and customs. As such they once more crossed the border, and succeeded in securing a trading site, and built themselves a house. They spent three years unquestioned, carrying on trade as a blind, but busying themselves night and day in studying the language and the people and making tentative translations of the Gospels into Thibetan.

At last they were suspected; they were found out. A squad of Thibetan soldiery came by order, and tore down their house before their eyes, and, handcuffing them, marched them across the border into China. They crossed the river which divides Thibet proper from Chinese Thibet, and were for carrying them on farther; but the missionaries refused to go farther, declaring that they were now within Chinese jurisdiction, and defying the Thibetan soldiery to force them farther. After a time the soldiery gave way and retired to their own country.

Father Andrew and his companions at once erected on the bank of the river, looking across into Thibet, a mission house and an orphanage and a press, and gathered in Thibetan boys to train and Christianize. Word came from the home authorities with reinforcements, large ones, and funds, and Father Andrew built eleven mission houses and had fourteen priests under his supervision, all working for Thibet, though not in it. An uprising took place. Their eleven houses were torn down and their schools scattered. Quietly he went to work and built in other places, still on the border, but in vain endeavoring to get in.

The powers at home then sent him orders, after fourteen years of unsuccessful effort to get in from China, to try India once more, and leaving the superintendency of the China mission in other hands, he sailed once more to Calcutta, and going up into the kingdom of Bhutan endeavored to get into Thibet from there. Again was he arrested and sent back into British India.

After various other unsuccessful attempts to enter Thibet from different points in the Himalayas, convinced at length that the time was not yet, he went up to the newly acquired British territory wedging in between the kingdom of Bhutan and the kingdom of Sikkim, and built a mission house there on the traders' route between Lhassa (Thibet) and Calcutta, and within thirty miles of the border of Thibet, and established a school for training boys in the Thibetan language and preparing them to enter Thibet as an army corps so soon as it should be open. There he has been for the last twelve years. It is a halting-place for Thibetan traders, who bring down thousands of horse-loads of wool for the Calcutta market, and week by week he talks with and preaches to these coming and going traders, and is trying to perfect himself in the dialects of all the different provinces of Thibet from which the traders come.

There I found him; there he poured into my ear, as that of a sympathizing fellow-missionary, the story of his life, an epitome of which I have given. He is now a gray-haired, emaciated man of sixty-two, but as full of enthusiasm for carrying the gospel into Thibet as when he arrived in Darjeeling thirty-six years ago; and his bright eyes kindled as he told me of the effort of his life, yet to be successful, because the work is of God and not of man.

He brought and laid in my lap, the fruit of twenty years' toil, a Thibetan-Latin dictionary of seven hundred pages of manuscript in his own handwriting, saying that this was the fifth and final revision, — the fifth time that he had written it all out with his own pen, — and that now, under orders from the Propaganda, he was just about going to Hong Kong, where they have a fine Thibetan press, to carry the dictionary through the press, that it might be a help to those missionaries of all nationalities who should enter Thibet, though perhaps he might not live to do so.

But, best of all, he had also in manuscript a perfected translation of the Gospel of John, which, in connection with his intercourse with the traders and travelers from all Thibet, he had been putting into such clear and idiomatic language as to be understood of all the people, which he was going immediately to print, so that, if he could not go into Thibet himself, he could send hundreds of these Gospels in by return traders, and so let the people of secluded Thibet know of Him who is the way and the truth and the life.

"Ah," said I to myself, as he showed me and told me this, " even a Roman Catholic missionary, who chooses the Gospel of John first to translate and scatter among the people,—that gospel that makes the most of the divinity and all-sufficiency of Jesus Christ and has the least to say of the Virgin Mary, — cannot but be a co-worker in bringing all these kingdoms into the one kingdom of Christ!"

What a lesson to some of us who complain of slow work and little success! Thirty-six years of foiled effort, and yet enthusiastic and hopeful as ever. God give us such stick-to-it-iveness!

XIX. Unhatchable Ink Bottles, or, Taught by a Hen.

YES, I have been taught by a hen this week, and the lesson has done me good.

You must know that the hens in India are members of the family. They live in the houses of the Hindus as much as the children. They feel perfectly at home, and the children pick them up in their arms as we would a kitten, and they have no hesitation in laying an egg in the best place in the house they can find. I have known of a native gentleman who took off his gold-bordered gauze turban and carefully placed it upside down on a mat in the corner of the room while he was eating his dinner, and when he rose and wished to put the turban on quickly, he found the pet hen quietly sitting in it, laying an egg.

But to return to my lesson. One of my young native assistants came in from his village, six miles out, where he is endeavoring to instruct a congregation of those who have lately renounced heathenism and placed themselves under Christian instruction, and presented the diary of his month's work for my inspection. For we wish to know in how many and in which of the surrounding heathen villages each native assistant has preached during the month, what chapters he has read and expounded to the new Christians at daily evening prayers in the school-house, and so on, in order that we may give the better counsel and direction for the next month. His diary was this time written in three different colors of ink. I asked the reason.

"Well, sir," said he, "you see our pet hen was determined to sit."

"Well, what then?"

"Why, we would not let her, and kept all the eggs out of her reach."

"Yes; goon."

"Well, sir, one morning — it was the 10th, for you see the color of the ink changes then — I came in from my morning preaching in a heathen village a mile north, and found that that hen had come in while my wife was in the kitchen, and jumped on to my low writing-desk, and scratched off the small brownstone ink-bottle into a corner. The ink had all run out; but there she was sitting on that bottle, determined to hatch that if we would not give her eggs. I had to fight to get it away from her, she was so resolved to sit on it. The ink was all gone, and as I had no more black ink I had to use blue."

"Well," said I, laughing, "how is it that a week later you changed again to red?"

"Why, you see, sir, I kept the blue-ink bottle hung up on the wall out of reach for a week, till I thought she had forgotten about it. At all events, I forgot, and went out one day and left this bottle open on the desk, just as I had been using it. And, sir, when I came back, there was the old hen with this ink-bottle under her in the same corner as before, and a streak of blue ink on the floor all the way up to the corner, and the bottle empty. I had nothing but red ink left in the house, and so I had to use that until I could come in here and get some more black ink."

"Well," said I, laughing again, "what have you done with the old hen?"

"Why, we thought that if she was so determined to sit we had better furnish her eggs to sit on. She is sitting on seven eggs in that very corner now."

"Well," said I, " she gained her point by a firm persistence in attempting to do her duty according to the light she had; and it is a lesson that you and I may well heed for ourselves."

I have thought it over a good deal since and I keep extracting comfort from it. We missionaries here in India have some very poor material to work upon, and some that seems to our eyes promising, and we do not know that it will not spring into life any more than Mistress Hen comprehended the fact that the ink-bottles would not hatch. We work on with zeal and earnestness; the Master sees our persistent effort, knows that it is perhaps fruitless on that material, and honors our purpose of service to Him by substituting more promising material.

There is a village of people fifteen miles from here for whose conversion I have worked hard for some years. I did think them promising, but they remain still unmoved and now seem almost as though they had no germ of life in them; but we have worked on. Today comes in word from five families, living a mile north of them, — of a higher caste and of much more intelligence, but among whom we had not worked except casually, — saying that they wish to embrace the religion of Jesus and be taught to follow Him. "Yes," said I, when the news reached me, "we have been, in our ignorance, perseveringly sitting on ink-bottles, and now God has given us eggs."

Does not many an earnest minister in Christian lands labor and pray and yearn for the conversion of certain individuals in his flock? And though these perchance remain cold and hard and lifeless, does not God often honor their earnest labor by sending to them other souls as seekers, of whom perhaps they have never thought?

How many lessons have I drawn from this incident for my own encouragement during the past week! But I will not delay to recount them. Every one who reads this story will be able to 'draw from it, perhaps, the very lessons which he most needs. Paul well summarizes one chief lesson when he says, "Let us not be weary in well-doing: for in due season we shall reap, if we faint not."

> "Sow in the morn thy seed;
>   At eve hold not thy hand;
> To doubt and fear give thou no heed;
>   Broadcast it o'er the land.
>
> "Thou canst not toil in vain;
>   Cold, heat, the moist and dry,
> Shall foster and mature the grain
>   For garners in the sky."

XX. Winding Up a Horse.

MANY years ago I bought in Madras a peculiar kind of horse; he had to be wound up to make him go.

It was not a machine, but a veritable live horse. When breaking him to go in the carriage he had been injured. An accident occurred in starting him the first time, and he was thrown and hurt and frightened. It made him timid, afraid to start. After he had once started he would never balk until taken out of the carriage. He would start and stop and go on as many times as you pleased, but it was very difficult to get him started at first each time he was harnessed to the carriage.

He .was all right under the saddle, an excellent riding horse, and would carry me long distances in my district work, so that I did not wish to dispose of him; but I could not afford to keep two; whatever I had must go in carriage as well as ride, and I determined that I would conquer.

How I have worked over that horse! At first it sometimes took me an hour to get him started from my door. At last, after trying everything I had ever heard of, I hit upon an expedient that worked.

I took a strong bamboo stick two feet long and over an inch thick. A stout cord loop was passed through a hole two inches from its end; this loop we would slip over his left ear down to the roots, and turn the stick round and round and twist it up.

It is said that a horse can retain but one idea at a time in its small brain. Soon the twisting would begin to hurt; his attention would be abstracted to the pain in his ear; he would forget all about a carriage being hitched to him, bend down his head, and walk off as quiet as a lamb. When he had gone a rod the horse-boy would begin to untwist, soon off would come the cord, and the horse would be all right for the day. The remedy never failed.

After having it on two or three times he objected to the operation, and would spring about and rear and twitch and back, anything but start ahead, to keep it from being applied. We would have, two of us, to begin to pat and rub about his neck and head; he would not know which had the key; all at once it would be on his ear and winding up. The moment it began to tighten he would be quiet, stand and bear it as long as he could, and then off he would go.

It never took thirty seconds to get him off with the key; it would take an hour without. After a little he ceased objecting to have it put on; he seemed to say to himself, " I have got to give in and may as well do it at once; " but he would not start without the key. In a few months he got so that as soon as we got into the carriage *he would bend down his head to have the key put on*, and one or two turns of the key would be enough.

Then the key became unnecessary. He would bend down his head, tipping his left ear to the horse-boy, who would take it in his hand and twist it, and off he would go.

My native neighbors said, "That horse must be wound up or he cannot run;" and it seemed to be so.

When he got so that the "winding up" was nothing but a form, I tried to break him of that, but could not succeed. I would pat him and talk to him and give him a little salt or sugar or bread, and then step quietly into the carriage and tell him to go. No. Coax him. No. Whip him. No. Legs braced, every muscle tense for resistance; a genuine balk. Stop and keep quiet for an instant, and he would hold down his head, bend over his ear, and look around for the horse-boy appealingly, saying very earnestly by his actions, "Do please wind me up; I can't go without, but I'll go gladly if you will." The moment his ear was touched and one twist given, off he would go as happy and contented as ever horse could be.

Many hearty laughs have we and our friends had over the winding up of that horse. If I were out on a tour for a month or two and he was not hitched to the carriage, or if he stood in the stable with no work for a week or two during the monsoon, a real winding up had to take place the first time he was put in. We kept him six years. The last week I owned him I had to wind him up. I sold the patent with the horse, and learned from the man that bought him that he had to use it as long as the horse lived.

I was thinking about that horse the other night, when it was too hot to sleep, and I suddenly burst into a laugh as I said to myself, "I have again and again, in the membership of our churches at home, seen that horse, that had to be wound up in all matters of benevolence."

I had often thought of that horse as I went through our churches at home in my visit to America in 1876, and imagined that I recognized him; but the whole thing came upon me with such peculiar force the other night that I must write out my thoughts.

There are some Christians — yes, I believe they are *Christians* — who have to be wound up by some external pressure before they will start off in any work of benevolence. Others will engage in some kinds of benevolence spontaneously, but will not touch other benevolent efforts unless specially wound up. Free under the saddle, but balky in carriage.

I knew of one good member of our church who would never give a cent to our Home Missionary Board unless he happened to hear of some missionary in the West who was actually without the necessaries of life, and then he would send in liberally. It took that to wind him up.

Another would never give to the board for educating young men for the ministry unless he happened to become acquainted with some candidate who was being aided; then his gifts would come in for helping that young man.

Another would never give to the Bible Society unless he chanced to hear of some particular town out West where but two Bibles could be found in a population of five hundred, although he knew perfectly well that there were hundreds of such communities, among whom the American Bible Society was daily endeavoring to introduce the divine Word. He must be wound up by a special case.

But it was especially of my visits through the churches in connection with our foreign missionary work that I was thinking when I said that I had so often recognized my horse that had to be wound up in all the different stages of his training.

Thank God, I found hosts of noble-hearted men and women all through the church, that needed no winding up; *whose conversion and consecration had extended down to their pockets;* who were always at the forefront in every good work; who required no spasmodic appeals. They give from a deep-set principle and an intelligent love for Christ and His cause, some even pinching themselves in the necessaries of life, as I know, to be able to give. It is on such that the security and continuance of our missions depend. We know that we can rely on them; they never fail us.

But there are others that have to be "wound up," willingly or unwillingly, before they will do anything in the missionary work. Some are very willing to be wound up.

"Domine," said a good elder who had just introduced himself to me one day, " I have come in on behalf of our church at ___ to see if you would not come out and give us a missionary talk. We ought to have sent in a collection to the Foreign Board months ago, but we have neglected it, and now we have been talking it over and have made up our minds to do something handsome if you will come out there and give us a talk."

"Well," said I, "I shall be very glad to come and tell you something of our work just as soon as I can edge a day in between other engagements. But if you have made up your minds to do something handsome for the board, why not do it at once and relieve their present pressing need, and I will come as soon as I can and give you the talk all the same."

"Oh no," said he; "we can't do that. We have made up our minds that we must give liberally, but we can start it easier if you come there and give us the talk first. You need not fear; we will give a good sum. That is settled, and it is mostly pledged; but you must come and talk to us first."

I smiled and said to myself, "There is my horse in its third stage of training. That church is bending down its ear and entreating me to twist it, for it has made up its mind to go, only it requires to be wound up first."

"Domine," said one of our earnest ministers to me, one Wednesday, " we raised one thousand dollars for the board last Sunday morning. It is more than usual and we are all happy over it. Now we want you to come over the first Sunday of next month and give us a missionary address."

"Good," said I; "that church has got one stage farther than my horse ever did in his training; for they start and do the work first, and bend down the ear to be twisted afterward." Did it not give me an earnest joy to go and tell that church what the Lord's war in India was and how much they had helped it?

A Sunday-school superintendent came to me one day with smiling countenance, saying, "Our Sunday-school has raised one hundred and seventy-five dollars during the past year for missions, and we have determined to give it to the work in India. The year closed three months ago and it is all in the hands of the treasurer; but we want you to come and give us a speech, and then it will be formally voted and sent at once to the board. We have been waiting all this time because they told us at the mission rooms that you were engaged up till now. When can yon come? The money is lying idle and we are waiting, and we know the board needs the funds; so come as soon as you can."

"Ah," said I, "everything is ready, and the family are in the carriage, but they have to sit there half an hour because the horse-boy is busy elsewhere, and the horse is holding down his ear all this time waiting for that particular horse-boy to come and twist it."

I was both pained and irresistibly amused by an incident that occurred not two hundred miles from New York, where the horse was in the first stage of training and stoutly resisted allowing its ear to be touched.

The missionary was announced to speak in the church on a given Sunday, when the annual collection would be taken up. A good member of the church — the pastor says a sincere Christian — was very much put out about it; had heard enough of these old missionaries and was not going to hear any more; did not believe in foreign missions; we had heathen enough at home.

The appointed Sunday came. Mr. A — and his family stayed away from church because they would not countenance the missionary address. They therefore missed the announcement which the pastor made, viz., that a telegram had been received that it was impossible for the missionary to be there; he would come next Sunday, and the annual collection would be deferred until then.

The following Sunday Mr. A — and family all filed into their pew, serene and happy in the thought that they had avoided the old missionary. As the organ was playing the voluntary the pastor entered the pulpit from the vestry, and a stranger with him. The pastor took the opening exercises, and the second hymn was sung, when the pastor rose and said that Mr. —, the missionary, as announced last Sunday, would now address them.

Mr. A — was thunderstruck; he did not like to go out in the middle of a service, and so determined to sit it through. The missionary told his simple tale. The plates came in; the collection was unprecedentedly large. Mr. A —'s plethoric pocket-book had disgorged itself upon the plates, and no heartier worker for foreign missions is found now in that church. Mr. A — had tried his best to keep his ear from being twisted; now it needs no twisting; he has learned to go and loves to go.

There was a church in our fold at home whose pastor was determined that it should not be wound up for foreign missions. He had succeeded, as he himself told me, in keeping all missionaries and secretaries and agents out of his pulpit during all the years of his pastorate. When the day came for collections for any of our boards, the fact was stated, the plates were passed, and those gave who wished. The collection, as a matter of course, under such a chill was a minimum.

It required some of the very best and most wary maneuvering to get hold of the ear of that church; but it was obtained and twisted, and off it started on the trot in the missionary work, and since then it has annually held down its ear and begged to have it twisted, as it wanted to go more.

Scores of incidents which occurred in my own experiences among the churches in America, and which recalled my " horse-winding," come crowding into my mind, but I forbear.

For I remember the phalanx of noble churches that needed no such winding up, who were all alive and always on the alert; who gave regularly, generously, nobly; who, from the pastor, the head, to the humblest member, prayed from the lips, from the heart, *from the pocket*, "Thy kingdom come." They are always glad to get hold of the recruiting watchman and ask him," Watchman, what of the night?" but they never have to be wound up to start them giving.

God give us more and more of such churches and more such Christians and church-members, so that no missionary or secretary need come to beg, but can come with radiant countenance and say, "Brethren, with the funds you are continually sending us for the work, we have done for the Master thus and thus." Then, in looking over our churches and our benevolent work, we shall no longer have occasion to remember "the horse that had to be wound up."

The Gopurams of a Hindu Temple.

XXI. Baptism of a Brahman.

A WEEK ago last Sabbath it was my privilege to baptize, in the Madanapalle church, a young Brahman of twenty-three years of age, who had been a seeker for a year and a half. His father is a Brahman priest, and long time teacher of a school in a town twenty-five miles west from here. The family is a family of school-teachers, his elder brother and all his uncles being teachers in different towns, and he himself has been a teacher of *payal,* or purely native, schools in different places.

We have some Christian village schools within a few miles of his town, and from them and their books, and from our preaching in the markets and fairs near there, and from Scriptures and tracts which we had scattered, he had learned more about Christianity and about Christ than his friends knew.

One year ago, after repeated and earnest talks with my colleague, Rev. William I. Chamberlain, and myself, he had decided to come out openly and embrace Christianity. He was then teaching in a school eight miles southeast of here, in the place of one of his uncles, who was absent on a few weeks' leave, and he promised that as soon as his uncle returned and released him he would come to Madanapalle, avow publicly his faith in Christ, and be baptized. Indeed, the Sabbath was appointed for his baptism; but he did not appear.

We for a time lost track of him. He was, it seems, induced to go and visit an uncle in the Mysore kingdom, who was priest and teacher; and that uncle succeeded in keeping him with him, on one pretext and another, until now. It was probably a part of the family plan to keep him away from us as far as possible; for while they did not know how earnestly he was seeking for the truth, they> did know that he often talked with our catechists and Christians, and they feared that he might be inclining toward Christianity.

A week ago, on Saturday, he arrived in town after his protracted stay in Mysore, dusty and footsore from his long journey on foot by a circuitous route to avoid being intercepted by his relatives, and found his way at once to the mission house. Our judicious and earnest catechist, John Souri, met him in the street on his way to the house, and after a good talk with him came with him to me, and we had a long, close, personal talk and prayer.

He was determined he would wait no longer. His examination for reception was thoroughly satisfactory. That evening he cut off his Brahmanical tuft of hair and his Brahmanical cord, and the marks of his deity on his forehead, which he had till then allowed to remain to avert suspicion, were removed, and he ate his evening meal with the catechist's family and slept there; and on Sabbath morning at our early morning service, with a face radiant with joy, he knelt and received the triune name upon his forehead, and was incorporated into Christ's visible church.

His old name had been the names of two of the Hindu gods. He asked for a new name, and took the name of Yákob John Ráyappa, the last being the Telugu for Peter, or "Rock," as he wished it to be known that he would stand firm as a rock in his new faith.

The church was crowded, many non-Christians being present to witness the baptism of a Brahman, for it had become known outside that it would take place.

It fell to me to conduct the service. I preached on " what Christ has done, does, and will do for His people." Among the non-Christians present was a Brahman of some thirty years of age, who has long been very near the kingdom of heaven. It is only his family that keeps him from coming out openly. The two whose attention was most intently — almost painfully intently — fixed upon the whole sermon as the subject developed itself, from Christ's determination in the eternal counsels to give Himself to save sinners down through the preparation, through His life and sacrificial death on earth, through His mediatorial intercessions for us in glory, until the final and complete coming of His kingdom, were the Brahman who had just received baptism, and whose face beamed with joy, and the Brahman who wanted, but dared not yet, to embrace Christ openly. He makes no secret of his belief in Jesus Christ as the Saviour of the world, but as long as he refrains from being baptized and breaking his caste his friends do not trouble him. He is not satisfied with his position, and we are not; he says he will come out openly for Christ ere long. Earnest and continued prayers are needed for such young men who wish to but dare not come out and take Jesus Christ as their Saviour. If effectual prayer is offered they will come.

XXII. BÍMGÁNI RÁMANNA, OR, UNRECKONED FRUITS.

BÍMGÁNI Rámanna is one who has been much in my thoughts and in my prayers for fifteen years. When the people of this hamlet — Timmareddipalle — came over to Christianity in July, 1872, and the Hindus and Mohammedans joined hands in persecuting the Christians and in trying to stamp out Christianity on its first entry into this region, Bímgáni Rámanna was the only high-caste Hindu of influence who cared and dared to stand out as our friend. He was the only landholder who dared sell us a piece of land on which to build our school-house church and our catechist's house. He sold us a nice site for a moderate price, and gave us some of the timber for building.

I now sit in the school-house church then erected on his land, and he has just been here to see me. He lives on the other side of the little sharp hill of granite rock at the foot of which our Christian village nestles; he is a high-caste farmer and landowner, a venerable white-haired old patriarch of seventy-five or eighty; his step is feeble and his eyes are growing dim.

News reached his house that I had come, — my first visit to these villages since returning from America in 1887, — and he came on foot a quarter of a mile, leaning on his staff, to see me, and I have been talking with him of Jesus and His salvation. My heart yearns toward him.

I had been to his village and presented the gospel of

Christ for their acceptance even before the people here came over to Christianity in 1872. He had listened with attention and interest; he seemed then drawn toward Christianity, at least so far as to wish to see those who embraced it fairly treated. The wrath of his neighbors came down on him because he sold us land and made it possible for us to build a church. He quietly bore their anger and continued his friendship with us.

It was only a few months after that that, one day, as I was dismounting from my pony at Timmareddipalle, having just ridden out from Madanapalle to see the people and preach to them, some men came running from Rámanna's village, saying that his eldest son had just had his foot fearfully gashed with an adz; that they could not stanch the flowing of the blood; that he was bleeding to death; that Rámanna had seen me riding across the fields, and had sent them to ask me to come quick and save his son's life.

In a few moments my pony had taken me to his house. Providentially I had my pocket surgical case with me. The arteries were taken up, the bleeding was stopped, his son lived, the foot was saved and healed. Then Rámanna turned upon his maligners, saying, " Now what have you to say? I sold the missionary some land, and he has saved my son's life." And no further objection could they make to his associating with us, even though I frequently went to his house and preached the gospel to him and his family and friends. Rámanna himself seemed always to listen to the truth with gladness, but none of his family appeared to sympathize with him, although treating me with politeness and attention.

To our successive catechists at Timmareddipalle and to our lower-caste converts Rámanna has all these fifteen years been a true friend, and has been, and continues to be, a frequent attendant upon our Sabbath services. Again and again through these years have I had earnest personal talks with him about openly embracing Christ, and so has our catechist, John Souri (now the Rev. John Souri), for whom he has a deep affection.

"I do believe in Jesus Christ as the Saviour of the world," he says, with apparently real sincerity; "I do believe that He alone can save us from our sins, that He alone can give eternal life, and I do want Him as my Saviour."

"Then, Rámanna, why not come out openly and embrace Him as your Saviour?"

"Oh, sir, look at my family. If they would come with me how gladly would I come; but not one of them would come. My wife, my three sons and their wives, my three daughters, my five grandchildren, would all desert and spurn me and drive me from the house. Even that I could bear if that were all. But though they cast me out to prove their devotion to their gods, the neighbors and all our relations would withdraw from all association with them. Not one of my younger daughters or granddaughters could marry a respectable Hindu, and, not becoming Christians, they would not and could not marry a Christian. My coming out would wreck my whole family, and they would have no comfort, as I do, in believing in Christ, for they do not believe in Him. How can I do it? No, sir, I must wait. Perhaps by and by they will come with me. If they do, what joy will it be to us all! If we come we must come together; I cannot come out alone."

"But, Rámanna, how can you wait? These fifteen years you have known about Jesus; now you are an old man; your eyes are dim, your hair is snow white, your steps totter. Do you not want Christ as your Saviour before you are called away?"

"Yes, sir; yes, I do want Him as my Saviour. Every day

I pray to Him. You know now I sit by the hour in the catechist's house and get him to read to me the stories of His life and suffering. For many years I have not prayed to any other god. Are you sure, sir, that He will not receive me unless I bring ruin on my whole family by openly embracing Him now? Wait a little, sir; I do believe my family are softening a little. Perhaps, ere many years, we can all come out together, and then what joy to us and you!"

Do you wonder that my heart yearns for the old man? Oh, power of the living God, come down and open the way for this old patriarch, yes, and for all his family, to embrace Thy Son as their Redeemer!

Missionary statistics are valuable; they show what progress we are making in gathering in acknowledged adherents into the church of Christ. But they do not tell all the work we do; they do not tell of all the souls that are sincerely moved with earnest desire for the salvation of Jesus Christ; for there are scores and perhaps hundreds of men around us who are in somewhat the same condition as dear old Bímgáni Rámanna. In all these cases our work has been fruitful to a certain extent, and of these the church should know and for these the church should pray; but still, as far as statistics go, they are all "unreckoned fruits."

XXIII. The Margosa Tree and the Hindu Temple

IWAS much interested in watching a contest between a margosa tree and a Hindu temple, in which the margosa tree bids fair to come off victor.

We are out on a preaching tour, preaching the gospel in the villages around the old Mohammedan fortress at Gurramkonda, where in former times the nawab of Gurramkonda ruled with an iron hand for so long a time. Joining with Tippu Sultan against the English, he fell about the same time as Tippu, — a century ago, — and his palace went to decay, or at least a part of it; but the better part has been preserved, and serves as a travelers' bungalow, and in that we are now abiding, as we are evangelizing the villages over which he once held sway.

The fort upon the high hill of Gurramkonda, or " horse mountain," used to be considered impregnable; but in the days of modern warfare it fell an easy prey to English shell and cannon, and in former years I used occasionally to come out here and spend a week or a fortnight in preaching in all the villages around. My work developed more in other quarters, and for nearly twenty years there has been no canvass of these villages. Now we are trying to give them once more the offer of life through Christ, and two of us missionaries are now in camp here with our native assistants, and are preaching through all these villages.

This morning we went out in the villages from two and

a half to five miles north. We had with us the record of my first tour in this region, in 1865. Against the name of the village in which John Souri and I preached this morning I find the entry, made in 1865, "Too much afraid to listen." Then they ran from us; this morning they gathered close around us.

We reached the village before sunrise, and found the people just astir. We sang one of the songs of Zion to a sweet Telugu tune, and soon had apparently the whole population of the village, old and young, male and female, gathered around us; and earnestly did they listen as we explained to them God's way of saving sinners. They placed a native couch out for us to sit upon, and all took their seats in a semicircle around us. We each spoke at length, and they not only listened through, but asked us many questions, and kept us for over an hour before they would let us go. We had a most interesting time. They had not heard the gospel sound for twenty years, and now they wanted to hear all about it.

As we were walking back we were talking about the growth, but the very slow growth, of Christianity in India and in our mission. We were speaking of its evidently having taken root in this region, and that it would stay and grow in spite of the arid surroundings, for it came of imperishable seed, when our attention was attracted to a firmly built Hindu temple by the side of the road between two villages, out of the roof of which was growing a beautiful margosa tree. We stopped to look at it.

The temple was of granite. Monolith pillars were placed at regular distances through it, and on these were resting long slabs of granite and *chunam* mortar, smoothed and polished on top, so as to form a perfectly waterproof roof that would last for centuries. From its west end rose its peculiar *gopuram*, or tower, common to Hindu temples. But out of the roof, at the junction of the tower, there was growing the margosa tree to which I have referred.

The margosa tree reached to the top of the gopuram. It would soon overtop it. Unless removed, it would unquestionably in time throw the temple to the ground. It had evidently sprouted and grown since I was here twenty years ago sowing the first gospel seed. Some monkey or some crow had carried the margosa fruit there to eat. A seed had dropped into a crevice. Some leaves had probably blown upon the temple, and, in the next monsoon covering it, had decayed and given nourishment to the sprouting seed. It had run a rootlet down into a small crack. By the aid of the casually blown leaves it had managed to live on. Another monsoon had helped it to secure firm foothold there in that unpropitious place, and year by year, undisturbed by any one, it has grown until it is a goodly tree, much more goodly than the temple out of which it is growing.

The temple seems to have been deserted. I presume, like many other Hindu temples, the funds which had been left by the one who in the fulfilment of a vow had built it had now been exhausted. The Brahmans of this age are not in the habit of keeping up worship in a temple where they are not paid for it. The temple is not, for Hindus, a place of gathering for instruction. The temple was deserted.

Passers-by might have climbed up and with a pinch of the fingers have pulled out the tree years ago; but no one did. What is every one's business is no one's business. It has not been molested; now it is a tree of size and strength. Its uprooting now would wreck the temple; if it lives its growing will wreck the temple. The temple was firmly built, and is strong; the tree is endowed with life, and is stronger. Massive temple must yield to living tree. Small in its beginning, but instinct with life and growth, it will prove the victor. Years are necessary, but the result is sure.

We had found our illustration without seeking for it. We thanked God for the parable. It was to me an inspiration, and I cannot refrain from recounting it for the encouragement of those who are helping us to plant the gospel seed in this apparently unpropitious soil. That temple represents Hinduism as it is now; it stands firm, defiant, the representative of a once more active religious spirit, but now without real life. It presents a tremendous resistance, but the resistance of the granite temple in the main. Here and there, now and then, it takes on life to oppose the new faith, hardly ever to propagate itself. Its chief power of resistance is in its massive inertness.

But the gospel seed is scattered. Some of it finds its way into unseen cracks and crevices; it is not noticed; no one takes the trouble to root it out. The gospel seed is germinating in thousands of unsuspected places. It is already, almost unnoticed, here and there towering over the gopurams of heathenism. Day by day are we introducing the seed into new crevices. Some will never take root. It has ever and everywhere been so. Some will grow. The heathen temples, all these shrines that exalt themselves between man and his Saviour, will crumble, and the tree whose leaves are for the healing of the nations will grow and blossom and fruit all through this sin-cursed land. I hear the voice wafted from the beautiful leaves of the margosa tree: "I will bring forth a seed out of Jacob, and out of Judah an inheritor of My mountains. . . . For as the days of a tree are the days of My people. They shall not labor in vain, ... for they are the seed of the blessed of the Lord." "His name shall endure forever: ... all nations shall call Him blessed. And blessed be His glorious name forever: and let the whole earth be filled with His glory. Amen, and Amen."